Loves Cruelty by James Shirley

A TRAGEDY. As it was presented by her Majesties Servants, at the private House in Drury Lane.

James Shirley was born in London in September 1596.

His education was through a collection of England's finest establishments: Merchant Taylors' School, London, St John's College, Oxford, and St Catharine's College, Cambridge, where he took his B.A. degree in approximately 1618.

He first published in 1618, a poem entitled Echo, or the Unfortunate Lovers.

As with many artists of this period full details of his life and career are not recorded. Sources say that after graduating he became "a minister of God's word in or near St Albans." A conversion to the Catholic faith enabled him to become master of St Albans School from 1623–25.

He wrote his first play, Love Tricks, or the School of Complement, which was licensed on February 10th, 1625. From the given date it would seem he wrote this whilst at St Albans but, after its production, he moved to London and to live in Gray's Inn.

For the next two decades, he would write prolifically and with great quality, across a spectrum of thirty plays; through tragedies and comedies to tragicomedies as well as several books of poetry. Unfortunately, his talents were left to wither when Parliament passed the Puritan edict in 1642, forbidding all stage plays and closing the theatres.

Most of his early plays were performed by Queen Henrietta's Men, the acting company for which Shirley was engaged as house dramatist.

Shirley's sympathies lay with the King in battles with Parliament and he received marks of special favor from the Queen.

He made a bitter attack on William Prynne, who had attacked the stage in Histriomastix, and, when in 1634 a special masque was presented at Whitehall by the gentlemen of the Inns of Court as a practical reply to Prynne, Shirley wrote the text—The Triumph of Peace.

Shirley spent the years 1636 to 1640 in Ireland, under the patronage of the Earl of Kildare. Several of his plays were produced by his friend John Ogilby in Dublin in the first ever constructed Irish theatre; The Werburgh Street Theatre. During his years in Dublin he wrote The Doubtful Heir, The Royal Master, The Constant Maid, and St. Patrick for Ireland.

In his absence from London, Queen Henrietta's Men sold off a dozen of his plays to the stationers, who naturally, enough published them. When Shirley returned to London in 1640, he finished with the Queen Henrietta's company and his final plays in London were acted by the King's Men.

On the outbreak of the English Civil War Shirley served with the Earl of Newcastle. However when the King's fortunes began to decline he returned to London. There his friend Thomas Stanley gave him help and thereafter Shirley supported himself in the main by teaching and publishing some educational works under the Commonwealth. In addition to these he published during the period of dramatic eclipse four small volumes of poems and plays, in 1646, 1653, 1655, and 1659.

It is said that he was "a drudge" for John Ogilby in his translations of Homer's Iliad and the Odyssey, and survived into the reign of Charles II, but, though some of his comedies were revived, his days as a playwright were over.

His death, at age seventy, along with that of his wife, in 1666, is described as one of fright and exposure due to the Great Fire of London which had raged through parts of London from September 2nd to the 5th.

He was buried at St Giles in the Fields, in London, on October 29th, 1666.

Index of Contents

To the Hopefull Paire of Nble Brothers, Cornet George Porter and Mr. Charles Porter.
LOVES CRUELTY
DRAMATIS PERSONAE
SCENE - Ferrara
LOVES CRUELTY
ACTUS PRIMUS
SCENE I - A Room in Clariana's House.
SCENE II - A Room in the Duke's Palace.
ACTUS SECUNDUS
SCENE I - Hippolito's Lodgings
SCENE II - A Room in the Duke's Palace.
SCENE III - Hippolito's Lodgings.
ACTUS TERTIUS
SCENE I - A Tavern.
SCENE II - A Room in Bellamente's House.
SCENE III - A Room in the Duke's Palace.
SCENE IV - A Room in Bellamente's House.
ACTUS QUARTUS
SCENE I - Clariana's Chamber.
SCENE II - A Room in the Palace.
SCENE III - A Room in Bellamente's House.
ACTUS QUINTUS
SCENE I - Hippolito's Lodgings.
SCENE II - A Room in Bellamente's House.
JAMES SHIRLEY – A CONCISE BIBLIOGRAPHY

To the Hopefull Paire of Noble Brothers, Cornet George Porter and Mr. Charles Porter

The knowledge of your growing virtues, have begot in all men love, in me admiration, and a desire to serve the manifold obligations I have to the true Example of worth Captaine Endemion Porter, instructed me to this presentation of my devoted respects to your noble selves, the true Ideas of his virtues. You are so equall in all the attributes of goodnesse, that it were a difficult indeavor for mee to distinguish betweene your perfections: Onely noble Captaine that prioraty which your birth has allowed you, ingages me in the first place to tender my service to your selfe, which I imagin'd could not have beene really accomplish'd, had I not joynd your brother in this act of my gratitude to you. Accept therefore heroicke paire of brothers, this tender of his best devotions to you who has no greater ambition then to be esteemed, the true servant of both your virtues W. A.

DRAMATIS PERSONAE

Duke of Ferrara
Bellamonte, a noble Gentleman
Bonaldo, an old Courtier
Hippolito, his son, an attendant on the Duke.
Sebastian, a private gentleman, enobled by the Duke.
Page to Hippolito
Groome to Hippolito
Courtiers
Servant to Bellamente
Fidler
Jugler
Drawer
Servants

Clairana, mistress, and afterwards wife, of Bellamente
Eubella, daughter of Sebastian
Milena, Clariana's Maid

SCENE

Ferrara

LOVES CRUELTY

ACTUS PRIMUS

SCENE I

A Room in Clariana's House

Enter **BELLAMENTE, CLARIANA**.

CLARIANA

You shanot goe, indeed you shanot.

BELLAMENTE
Lady.

CLARIANA
Vnlesse the fault of your poore entertainment.

BELLAMENTE
Nay now you trespasse, and dishonour me
With a suspition that I can be so
Vnjust, as not to acknowledge, you haue made
A free, and liberall welcome—but excuse.

CLARIANA
Love shall supply, what else hath beene defective,
To expresse my thankes for your kind visit.

BELLAMENTE
Tis
Businesse that now ravish me away
By this white hand, which but to kisse, would tempt me
To dwell an age here, I must waite vpon
The Duke.

CLARIANA
Why so you may.

BELLAMENTE
Tis now my time.

CLARIANA
You are not tied to such a strict obseruance
That halfe an houre can preiudice you, come
I know you may dispence with dutie so much.

BELLAMENTE
You may command;

CLARIANA
Not any thing that shall
Reflect iniurious to your selfe.

BELLAMENTE
I know
You have more charity.

CLARIANA

If there be other
Cause, that concernes your honor, or your fortune,
Trust me, I would not by a minites stay
be guilty of your wrong, and yet me thinkes
If there were any thing you might tell me;
There's not a thought, that I dare keepe from you,
No sigh but you may know from whence it breakes,
I haue not had a teare, but you haue searchd
The very spring, come ist some other friend?

BELLAMENTE
O doe not so farre wound your servant Madam
To thinke my heart can allow any time
For the imagination of another
Woman, did all the goodnesse of the sexe
Conspire in one without you, I should loue
My first election, and be blest to write
All my devotion here; if by the title
Of friend, you vnderstand a man, there is
But one in the whole world I dare call friend,
And I am confident it would trouble me
As much to find a cause that would offend him
As to be guilty of the sinne.

CLARIANA
Hippolito.

BELLAMENTE
If he expected me a day, the crime
Were easily purg'd, I can presume on him.

CLARIANA
This is but little of that Character
I haue heard your tongue deliuer, if his loue
Be what you often haue proclaimd, trust me
He is a treasure.

BELLAMENTE
Such as both the Indies
Sha'not buy, from me.

CLARIANA
Whatthing's rare in him
'Bove other friends?

BELLAMENTE
His love, his love Clariana.

CLARIANA
That may be found in many

BELLAMENTE
But not so rich of so exact a nature
All other is but drossie;

CLARIANA
He will venture
His life to aduance your cause

BELLAMENTE
He has don't often
But that is not the thing for which I bosome
Hippolite, I can returne full weight
Of blood for his, engage my selfe to dangers
As high and horrid as he can for me,
But every daring fellow in the street
Can draw a sword, and will for his gay honour
Which swaies him more then his religion,
I'th field maintaine a good or impious quarrell:
But he is such a one to me, the name
Of friend's too narrow for him, and I want
A word that carries more divinitly
To expresse his love.

CLARIANA
You are not nice to extoll him,
What has he done?

BELLAMENTE
An act above all friendship
That yet had story, bov'e all recompence
I am not capable of a cause, to quit
His unexampled virtue.

CLARIANA
This is strange.

BELLAMENTE
You will acknowledge when you heare it, and
It does concerne you somewhat.

CLARIANA
Me, pray let not
My ignorance make me so vnhappy, not
To give my thankes if he hath aym'd apat
Of curtesie to me, what ist?

BELLAMENTE
He dares not see thee.

CLARIANA
Dares not see me why
Am I so terrible? does he feare I shall
Transforme him? sure Minerva never drest
My haires, he should imagine I present
Medusa to him, dares not see me? I
Shoot no infection, nor breath any mist
That shall corrupt him, whats his reason pray?

BELLAMENTE
Because I love thee, I ha courted him
As some would do their mistresse, but to be
Companion of one visit, and his love
Would not permit him.

CLARIANA
Not to see your friend.

BELLAMENTE
He loves me so well, that he dares not trust
His frailty with thy sight, whom I have so
Commended, least before our marriage
Some thing should share in his affection
Which he hath studied to preserue intire
For me, he will not trust his eyes with any
Beauty I loue, least they should stray with too much
Licence, and by degrees corrupt his faith
He knowes not what may theiue upon his seness
Or what temptation may rise from him.
To undoe us all.

CLARIANA
A rare and noble friendship.

BELLAMENTE
Ist not Clariana?

CLARIANA
He need not feare I shall
Commit a rape upon his friendship, and
A love so just and perfect as his, cannot
With one sight of a woman, armd with more
Beauty then mine, be violated;
He dares not trust his frailty, he has faults

Belike though he be such a miracle
In friendship, pray enioy him, and by no meanes
Tempt his soft nature to a crime so great
As seeing me, it shall suffice my love's
To thee inviolable, and what opinion
For your sake, I may modestly allow
The man I never saw, because your friend
Be confident he has it.

BELLAMENTE
Thar't all sweetnesse
But I forget my attendance on the Duke
Now you allow my absence, vertuous thoughts
Streame in your bosome.

CLARIANA
Not one kisse at parting?

BELLAMENTE
Let one speake the devotion of your servant
That would but dares not stay, to print a thousand.

[Kisses her. Exit.

CLARIANA
Milena.

[Enter **MILENA**.

MILENA
Madam.

CLARIANA
Is Bellamente gone?

MILENA
Yes Madam

CLARIANA
I must see this strange friend, bid make ready
The Caroch, and do attend—

MILENA
I shall

[Exit.

CLARIANA

Dares not trust his frailty with a woman! a fine fellow!

[Exit.

A Room in the Duke's Palace.

[Enter **HIPPOLITO**, **COURTIER**.

HIPPOLITO
Eubella come to Court?

COURTIER
This morning Sir
And much grac'd by the Duke, Sebastian
Her father made a Knight.

HIPPOLITO
A Knight? Wy much good doot him, hee's a gentleman may deserve it for his daughters sake. The Duke has the advantage, he is able to make great men, there is no bande to a round pension per annum, or the severe brow of authority, promotion will turne the stomack, we under-sinners o'the commonwealth, ha nothing but our good parts to procure for us, she is like to become game royall then.

COURTIER
The Duke pretends she shall be in some place neere the Duchesse.

HIPPOLITO
In some neere place with the Duke, when the Duchesse is in another bed and never Dreames on't; she may in time be a gamster, in the meane time the Duke will play at Cards with her, and if he chance turne up a coate, the honor shall be hers, and a stock perhaps to set up the precious sinne withall, is she not yet Ladified?

COURTIER
She is in the way to rise

HIPPOLITO
Thou art mistaken, she is in the way to fall, a hansome Gentle woman and new come to Court, in the high way to fall too, if any thing will doot, the Duke has taken a course to take in her Maiden towns.

COURTIER
Did not you love her?

HIPPOLITO

No faith, I cannot properly say I did ever love her, she was too honest, if she have praid since, she has beene sorry for loving me so well,—she was too wise to be a whoore, and I was not so much a foole to marry, till my time were come,

COURTIER
What time?

HIPPOLITO
Why the fall of the leafe, when my Summer is over, the Dog-days may do much wo me, marry before one and thirty? a solescisme, tis more honorable to be a peepe out, then stand at a single game, tis neither Courtly nor fashionable, and whats become of her wise brother?

COURTIER
He cannot do amisse in the generall aduancement, if his father and sister rise—

HIPPOLITO
He must needs shew a high forehead, tis such a dog in a wheele, hee'le never become a doublet in fashion, he talkes as if he had read Poetry out of Almanacks, and makes a leg like a Farmer, I wonder who begot him?

COURTIER
His father.

HIPPOLITO
What father? It had beene a question, had his mother beene a Courtier, and not liv'd and died honest in the Country, they that looke upon him, and his sister, would never think two, Pollux and Helena, twinnes, i'th same egge, yet she may be a good hen hereafter and lay, but and he be not addled, he is wiser then his nurse tooke him for

COURTIER
Will you not see 'em in?

HIPPOLITO
Where are they?

COURTIER
I'th garden where the Duke hath beene this halfe houre in private discourse with her

HIPPOLITO
No Ile backe agen, I ha not eaten to day, and I dare not looke upon an honest woman fasting, tis ominous, and we have too many fishdayes already, if the Duke aske for me make some excuse.

[Going.

COURTIER
I owe my preferment to you, and you may challenge my services,

[Enter **BELLAMENTE**. ·

BELLAMENTE
Friend whither in such hast

HIPPOLITO
If thou lov'st me interrupt me not, I dare not stay, there are new things at Court, and I ha not provided a complement yet Ile see thee anon.

[Exit.

BELLAMENTE
Farewell. Wild as the wind some crochet has possest him
And he is fixt to follow't he but wants
A litle pruning, and no Courtier
Could grow up more accomplisht, I could wish him
An ounce or two of snow to qualifie
Some fury in his blood, were there no women
He would be a brave man, but why do I
Trouble my selfe, that am secure? the Duke.

[Enter **DUKE** leading in **EUBELLA**, **SEBASTIAN**, **BONALDO**, **COURTIERS**.

DUKE
You are too modest

EUBELLA
That was not wont to be a vice my Lord
Or if it be too homely for the Court
And out of fashion, with your highnes pardon
I shall be welcome with it, to the place
I came from.

SEBASTIAN
Hold that constant my Eubella.

DUKE
Will you still be ignorant?

BONALDO
Is not that your daughter?

SEBASTIAN
She was.

BONALDO
Has she found another father?

SEBASTIAN

She has found a miserie.

BONALDO
Let them tell the markes that lost it and take it agen
By my consent.

DUKE
Bellamente.

BELLAMENTE
My Lord.

DUKE
Is she not an excellent creature, wer't not pitty
That so much beautie should be cast away
Vpon a thanklesse woman?

BELLAMENTE
How sir?

DUKE
That wonot use it to her best advantage?
I have beene courting this houre for
A smile.

BELLAMENTE
I like not this.

SEBASTIAN
Nor I.

BELLAMENTE
I cannot but congratulate your good fortune.

SEBASTIAN
Do not, do not
You ever have beene held an honest man.
Pray, do not mock me, it has pleas'd his grace
To give, me a new name; a riban in my forehead.

BONALDO
Sebastian's a forehorse-but would I were to be the Dukes taster.

SEBASTIAN
But there's a price too great set for the honor,
That is my daughter sir, and though I say't
She is yet a virgin, would you part with such
A child to buy a Kinghthood? bribe at such

Expence for a poore title?

BELLAMENTE
Tis darke language
I dare not understand you, but you may
Mistake the Duke.

SEBASTIAN
I wod I did, the way
To be assurd is to aske the question sir.

DUKE
Sebastian you put us well in mind, we have forgot
You have too litle testemonie of our favour
You shall be Captaine of our Guard.

BONALDO
Howes that? the Duke does love her, I hope not Honestly, she was not borne to he a Dutchesse, I have it Heaven forgive us, the Duke meanes to make her owne father the Pander, tis so, he does not use to give such offices for nothing, well go thy wayes for a princely Ferret, she cannot hold out upon these termes.

SEBASTIAN
I know not what to say, but do you thinke
She shall be safe here, is the Court a Sanctuary
For virgins?

BONALDO
Tw'ere better you were both pickeld.

SEBASTIAN
It depends upon the Princes chastity
Whose example builds up vertue
Or makes iniquity a trade

DUKE
Why should you
Be such an enemy to your selfe, come faire one
Thinke who it is that Courts you, he that may Command.

EUBELLA
My life but not my honor.

DUKE
Your honor? why I offer in exchange
A thousand.

EUBELLA
But not all of value, to

Repurchase mine, when I have sold it to
Your wantonnesse, remember sir how much,
You may by one black deed, make forfeit of,
Your precious eternity.

DUKE
No doctrines.

EUBELLA
Warrant not so much ill by your example
To those that live beneath you, if you suffer,
That sordid vice raigne in your blood, who shano't
Be afraid to live with vertue

DUKE
Let a kisse correct this vnkind language.

BONALDO
I want patience to see any man kisse
A hansome Gentlewoman, and when my owne lips
Cannot use their owne priviledge, I prophesie what Will
Become on her, for all her modesty, but dare stay
No longer the sight of so much temptation.

[Exit.

SEBASTIAN
Why should any
Promotion charme my honest tongue? Ide rather
Plough my owne acres with my innocence
Then have my name advanc'd by poisoned honor,
He must not Whoore my daughter

BELLAMENTE
I commend.
Your noble soule, but be advis'd how you
Expresse your trouble, griefe while it is dumb
Doth fret within, but when we give our thoughts
Articulate sound we must distinguish hearers,
Princes are dangerous and carry death
Vpon their tongue, I wish you well and speake
My friendly counsell—'las poore gentleman!

DUKE
Come you must weare this Iewell, I ha don,
But you must live at Court.

EUBELLA

You will be just
To your owne honor, and not give me cause
To curse your entertainement

DUKE
Y'are too scrupulous.

SEBASTIAN
Great sir.

DUKE
Give order for his Patent to be drawne
We will create him Lord, no honor can
Reward your merit, and the title will
Become the father of this excellent maide

COURTIER
His mouth's stopd agen.

2ND COURTIER
Lord? What does the Duke meane?

1ST COURTIER
No harme to the Gentlewoman.

2ND COURTIER
If these wonot purchase the old mans consent to leave his Daughter to his highnesse mercie, for he rises
that she may be humbled, there are other courses to be thought on, Sebastian has beene a Souldier,
there are quarrells now in the world and Christian warres he were a fit man for a Generall when hee's
abroad, the siege at home wonot be so desperate.

1ST COURTIER
She must be the Court Starre:

2ND COURTIER
Do not you blaze it abroad neither, I do not
Thinke his grace will acquaint his counsell
With such a cause.

3RD COURTIER
The old man for ought I see has no stomack to it.

DUKE
Wheres Hippolito?

1ST COURTIER
I see him this morning.

DUKE
He is an active Courtier, practis'd in these amorous
Paths, weele try his skill to winne her to our
Close embrace, command him presently waite on us
Bellamente.

SEBASTIAN
We heare you are to be married.

EUBELLA
Ill tell you more hereafter
I do not like the Court, and yet I have
His royall word no force shall touch my chastity.

SEBASTIAN
Be resolute for thy honor, I weigh not
The titles he would heape, remember girle
Thy mothers vertue, since thy birth, though noble
Cannot expect his Courtship for thy selfe,
Scorne to be cald a Lady for his pleasure

[Enter **BONALDO**

DUKE
Signior Bonaldo, wheres your sonne?

BONALDO
So please your highnesse hee's not ith Court
Vnlesse he be in some o'the lobbyes, I could
Not examine all: Ha! tis come about, and the
Father Ile lay my life is laying the law to her,
Why was not I a Duke, I have as many titillations, though I be the elder huntsman.

DUKE
You would not thanke us for
A law, that none about our Court should marry ere we
Choose a wife our selfe.

BELLAMENTE
Your grace is pleasant.

DUKE
Tell me what hast heard of that Eubella?

BELLAMENTE
A very noble character.

DUKE

What doe you call noble?

BELLAMENTE
Shee's chaste and virtuous

DUKE
A vertuous folly but we let her coole
Too much; Eubella

SEBASTIAN
I know not, still I feare her innocence
Is not enough to guard her, if the Duke
Pursue her vitiously, what is a virgin
Against so many flattering temptations?

DUKE
Come fairest.

SEBASTIAN
I would you would be pleasd my Lord

DUKE
I am infinitely pleasd my Lord, with that rare modesty
Sets on this cheeke, and with thy selfe whom we
Have not yet grac'd sufficiently, our state
Doth want such able honest men, and we
Admit you to our high and secret counsels;
I prophesie the Dukedome shall owe much
To your care, and grave directions.

[Exeunt all but **SEBASTIAN** and **BONALDO**.

BONALDO
Hayda a Privy Counselor too.
We are like to have fine smock-age ont, virgins will be virgins
If the Duke hold this humour and at such price forestall the market;
A widow will be excellent meat againe; hee's Melancholy,

SEBASTIAN
Shall I be choakd with honors and not speake?
Where is my courage, shall a few gay titles
Corrupt a father? Bovaldo thou art reported a
Good fellow.

BONALDO
Would you were as right for your owne sake:

SEBASTIAN

Is there no tricke to give a man a spirit?
I would be valiant; I dare not talke;

BONALDO
If you have a mind to quarrell drinke.

SEBASTIAN
Well thought on, that shall arme me against all
His flattery shall's to a Tauerne?

BONALDO
Ile beare you company

SEBASTIAN
It shall be so; the Courts too open,
You shall command Sebastian

BONALDO
My Lord—

SEBASTIAN
No titles, Ile thither to forget em and drinke my selfe into a heate above his conjuration, if there be a
spirit in wine Ile swallow it: How is man falne; that to preserue his name and defend innocence must fly
to shame.

BONALDO
Ile lead you sir.

ACTUS SECUNDUS

SCENE I

Hippolito's Lodgings

[Enter **HIPPOLITO**, **FENCER**.

HIPPOLITO
Come on sir.

FENCER
Pretty well I protest la, keepe your guard, now sir

HIPPOLITO
What de'e thinke ont, I shall never hit your subtle body

FENCER

A very dextrous profer, bring it home, everwhile you live
Bring your weapon home,

HIPPOLITO
Agen sir

FENCER
But you do not hit me the neat Schoole-way,
I wont give a rush to be kil'd out of the Schoole-way, you must
Falsifie thus.

HIPPOLITO
How now man?

FENCER
Pretty well, let us breath

[Enter **PAGE** and whispers to his **MASTER**.

HIPPOLITO
A Gentlewoman?

PAGE
That has woed me sir, if it were possible, to see you first
At some distance

HIPPOLITO
Is she hansome?

PAGE
I am no comeptent judge of beauty, but if you will have
My verdit, she is guilty of a good face.

HIPPOLITO
Ile trouble you no more, I thanke you for this exercise

FENCER
The tother bout

PAGE
Faces about good, Master Fencer, my Master has some businesse
You and I will trie a veine below

FENCER
I would have another thrust I protest

PAGE
Not downe staires, what if my master desire to try his skill

With some body else.

[Exit.

[Enter **CLARIANA**.

HIPPOLITO
What means the Gentlewoman? I am not to be bought Lady.

CLARIANA
If you were I have not wealth enough to purchase you.

HIPPOLITO
Do not over value me neither.

CLARIANA
I would I had not seene him

HIPPOLITO
Have you businesse with me Lady?
Expect me in the next roome.

CLARIANA
I came sir but to see you

HIPPOLITO
To see how I doe, why I thanke you, you are pretty, and I
Am'well, what and they were both put together

CLARIANA
You may accuse my modesty that thus rudely,—

HIPPOLITO
Nay Lady, you cannot offend me that way, I can be as
Rude as you—

CLARIANA
What shall I say? d'ee know me sir?

HIPPOLITO
No good faith not I, but I shall desire to know you any way
You please

CLARIANA
Did you never see me?

HIPPOLITO
See you? you have a beauty would challenge a remembrance

But sure I was not so happy till this minute

CLARIANA
You are a Courtier and can flatter.

HIPPOLITO
And such beauty was made to be flattered

CLARIANA
Tis a signe it carries not merit enough along to justifie it
But tis as it is, I cannot help it, yet I could paint if I list

HIPPOLITO
The more excellent, I do not love your artificiall faces▪ give
Me one that dates blush, and have but her owne colour for't
Her'es a cheeke hath both Creame and Strawberie s••'t a lip with
Cheeries that say come eate me.

CLARIANA
You are very bold

HIPPOLITO
Not so bold as you are welcome, you say you came to see me
And I would satisfie more then one of your sences. I do not
Know your name,

CLARIANA
What would you do with it, if I told you?

HIPPOLITO
Lay it up precious to memory, and open it as a relick for
Men to do it reverence, at my crowned table drinke a health
To the excellent owner, and call it my everlasting Valentine.

CLARIANA
You would not

HIPPOLITO
By this kisse but I would;

CLARIANA
No swearing

HIPPOLITO
I cannot take too deepe an oath in such briske claret,
Say shall I know it Lady?

CLARIANA

Excuse me sir
I would not have my name be the tost for every cup of Sack You drinke, you wild Gallants have no mercy upon Gentlewomen, when you are warme ithe Canaries

HIPPOLITO
Why conceale it, I am not in love with a name, and yet I have a Grudging, asuspition, that you ha paund or lost it

CLARIANA
What?

HIPPOLITO
Your good name, but let it go, I can tarry 'till you recover it, I have a bed with in Lady, and a Couch.

CLARIANA
What to do?

HIPPOLITO
Nothing but to laugh and ly downe:

CLARIANA
You are very merry sir. I do like him infinitly, I came for no such purpose, I am not so weary but I can walke

HIPPOLITO
There is a Gallery to walke after.

CLARIANA
I find it true, what you are reported;

HIPPOLITO
Leave this impertinency, and resolue me agen what you
Came hither for

CLARIANA
If you will have the truth, I heard you had a wit, and
A tall one, and I came hither

HIPPOLITO
To take it downe,

CLARIANA
To try the keenesse, I confesse it has a pretty edge ont, not altogether so sharpe as a rasor

HIPPOLITO
Very good, I shall love this periwinke.

CLARIANA

They say you love women too

HIPPOLITO
So they, say, but dare not ly with e'm

CLARIANA
I do not beleeve you can love any woman truly, that love so many

HIPPOLITO
Be like you hold some intelligence in my affaires, and have a
Catalogue of all my gennets, I thinke there be some women
In the world that wish me well, and shan't I
Love 'em againe?
The misery on't is, I have never a Mistresse

CLARIANA
Do you not confesse many?

HIPPOLITO
Women I grant, some moveables, trimmings for a chamber things that serve the turne, but never a
mistresse one that I would love and honor above all, my Lady Paramount, and super-intendent
Lindabrides and such an Empresse would thou wert.

[Enter **PAGE**.

PAGE
Sir one from the Duke

HIPPOLITO
The Duke; Lady Ile waite upon you presently.

CLARIANA
I dare not name his friend nor who I am
All is not well within me.

HIPPOLITO
Say I attend his grace immediately, Lady pardon my former rude trespasses, how unwelcome the cause
is that must divorce me from your sweet company I can onely imagine, but if you dare be so gracious,
having already so much honord me to entertaine the time of my absence in that gallery, where some
Pictures may help away the time, you will oblige in the highest degree your servant, as I am a
Gentleman I will returne instantly, and acknowledge the infinite favors:

CLARIANA
The worst is past already, and I am desperately engag'd
I have not yet exprest the businesse sir
That brought me hither, confident of your noblenesse
I will expect a while,
Pray send my servant to me

Good fortunes w'ee

HIPPOLITO
I must not loose her yet,
Lady with your pardon, you shall keepe possession a while,
This key will secure you till my returne.
I hope it will be a fashion shortly for Gentlewomen to come home and take their tribute, it will be some reliefe to our landresses.

Venus grant me a speedy returne,
And she scapes me very hard if she have not her come againe.

[Exeunt.

SCENE II

A Room in the Duke's Palace.

[Enter **DUKE, BELLAMENTE, EUBELLA, COURTIERS.**

DUKE
Yet Lady have you changd your resolution
May I now hope to be admitted?

EUBELLA
Whether?

DUKE
To your embraces

EUBELLA
Sir I dare not tell you
What I would say, I would some other man
Might pleade your argument, I should be plaine
And bolder in my answer, in your person
There's something makes me fearefull to expresse
What is behind, another in your name
Would more encourage me to speake.

DUKE
I'me glad,
I have provided for your modestie
I wonder hee's so tedious—

EUBELLA
Whither will these libidnous flames of men.

Pursue poore virgins? does a generall feaver
Possesse their blood? who shall protect the chast?

[Enter **HIPPOLITO**.

HIPPOLITO
When would you have me doot?

DUKE
Now she is in presence.

HIPPOLITO
I am not so well
Fortified as I may be an houre hence

DUKE
It must not be delaid, I will prepare her.

HIPPOLITO
I am undone, the poore Gentlewoman will be in Purgatory when she finds I ha lock'd her up, and how to release her I know not, no tricke, no device? Bellamento prethee friend go to my lodging, and with this key release a Gentlewoman, that expects my returne, the Duke has put a scuruy businesse upon me, kisse her hand for me, and excuse my stay, wot? tell her hereafter I hope we shall meet and not be distracted, my honor is in pawne.

BELLAMENTE
You dare trust me with your tame foule belike, for once
Because there is necessity, Ile take some compassion a your
Pigions, yet you refusd to see my Mistresse, d'ee remember?

HIPPOLITO
No quittance now.

DUKE
This is the man Lady, d'ee start already? winne her to the Game —

HIPPOLITO
Ile do what I canne; I may have better luck for you then
For my selfe, give us opportuniy.

EUBELLA
Has the Duke pointed him to be his orator.

HIPPOLITO
Lady I bring you newes, which you must welcome,
And give me thanks for,

EUBELLA

If they be worthy.

HIPPOLITO
The Duke loves you.

EUBELLA
D'ee know sir what you say?

HIPPOLITO
I am not drunke, the Duke, I say does love you.

EUBELLA
Oh do not use that modest name of love
To apparrell sinne, I know you meant to tell me
The Duke pursues me with hot lust.

HIPPOLITO
You are a foole,
You understand his meaning, will you be wise, and meet it? such favours are not offred to every body, I
ha knowne as hansome a Lady as you, would ha given all the world, and her selfe too for a bribe to any
man that would ha procured her but a kisse, nay as honest women no dispraise ha longd for't, and it was
mercie in his highnesse to save the childs nose, you have the whole treasure presented to you, Jupiter in
a golden shower falling into your lap intreats to be accepted, come
You must receive him.

EUBELLA
Whom?

HIPPOLITO
The Duke

EUBELLA
Withall the duty of a servant.

HIPPOLITO
Thats well said.

EUBELLA
If he bring vertuous thoughts along with him

HIPPOLITO
Bring a Fiddlestick, come you do not know what it is to be a Dukes Mistresse, to enjoy the pleasures
o'the Court to have all heads bare, the knees bow to you, every doore fly open as you tread, with your
breath to raise this Gentleman, pull downe that Lord, and new mold the tother Lady, weare upon a tire
the wealth of a province, have all the fashions brought first to you, all Courtiers sue to you, Tilts and
Turnaments for you; to have the aire you live in, nay your very breath perfumd, the pavement you tread
upon kisst, nay your Dog, or Munkey, not saluted without an officious leg, and some title of reverence.
Are you Melancholy? a Maske is prepared, and Musicke to charme Orpheus himselfe into a stone,

numbers presented to your eare that shall speake the soule of the immortall English Ionson, a scene to take your eye with wonder, now to see a forrest move, and the pride of summer brought into a walking wood, in the instant as if the sea had swallowed up the earth, to see waves capering about tall ships, Arion upon a rocke playing to the Dolphins, the Tritons calling up the sea-Nimphes to dance before you: in the height of this rapture a tempest so artificiall and suddaine in the clouds, with a generall darkenes and thunder so seeming made to threaten, that you would cry out with the Marriners in the worke, you cannot scape drowning, in the turning of an eye, these waters ravish into a heaven, glorious and angelicall shapes presented, the starres distinctly with their motion and musick so inchanting you, that you would wish to be drowned indeed, to dwell in such a happinesse.

EUBELLA
Fine painted blessings!

HIPPOLITO
Will you feast, the water shall be summond to bring in her finny and shell inhabitants, the aire shall be unpeopled, and the birds come singing to their sacrifice, Banquets shall spread like wildernesses, and present more variety then men can possibly take in surfets. Are you sicke? all the Court shall take phisick for you, if but your finger ake, the Lords shall put on night-caps, and happiest that Courtier that can first betray how much he suffers with you. Doth not this Pallace please, the Court remoues to morrow: doth the Scituation distast, new places are built, and piramids to put downe the Egyptians: will you hunt to day? the game is provided and taught newes to delight you: will you take the pleasure of the River? the Barge attends, Musicke and the Marmaides go a long, Swannes dy a long the shores and sing their owne dirges: will you spend? the Exchequer is yours all honor and offices yours, and which is the crowne of all, the Duke himselfe is yours, whose ambition shall be to make those pleasures lasting, and every day create new ones to delight his Mistresse.

EUBELLA
And yet I thinke you would not give away
Your right hand for all these, much lesse present
A poniard to your heart and stab your selfe.

HIPPOLITO
I thinke I should not.

EUBELLA
And would you tempt me to do worse?

HIPPOLITO
Worse?

EUBELLA
To sell my honor basely for these vanities.

HIPPOLITO
Vanities?

EUBELLA
Meere trifles.

HIPPOLITO

And you go to that Lady, that which you part withall for
All these pleasures, is but a trifle.

EUBELLA

What?

HIPPOLITO

Your maidenhead? where is it? who ever saw it? Is it a thing in nature? what markes has it? many have
beene lost you'ld say, who ever found em'? and could say and iustifie, this is such or such a womans
maidenhead? a mere fiction, and yet you thinke you have such a jewell on't.

EUBELLA

You cannot be so ignorant as you seeme.

HIPPOLITO

I tell you what I thinke.

EUBELLA

Is chastity and innocence no treasure?
Are holy thoughts and virgin puritie
Of so small value? where is your religion?
Were we created men and women to
Have a command and empireore the creatures
And shall we loose our priviledge our charter
And wilfully degrad our selves of reason
And piety, to live like beasts, nay be such?
For what name else can we allow our selves?
Hath it been held in every age a vertue
Rather to suffer death then staine our honor?
Does every sinne stricke at the soule and wound it
And shall not this, so foule as modesty
Allowes no name, affright us? can the Duke
Whose wicked cause you plead, with justice punish
Those by his lawes that in this kind offend,
And can he thinke me Innocent, or himselfe
When he has plaid the foule adulterer?
Princes are gods on earth and as their virtues
Doe shine more exemplary to the world
So they stricke more immediately at heaven
When they offend.

HIPPOLITO

I did not trouble you with this divinity,

EUBELLA

I see you are a Gentleman he favours

Be worthy of his trust, and counsell him
To better wayes, his shame is your dishonor;
For every good man suffers with his prince:
Put him in the memory of the holy vow,
When he received his Septer
He promis'd then protection to the innocent;
Tell him the punishment in store for lust
This were an Angels office.

HIPPOLITO

But Ile not doo't for a hundred angells, thanke you as much
As though I did, that were the tricke of a wise Courtier, tell
The Prince of his faults.

EUBELLA

If he have but the seeds of goodnesse in him
Hee'll take it well

HIPPOLITO

He shall doe when I take it upon me,
I am not weary o'my place, thou wodst make a very fine Court
Surgeon—well dee heare, you wo'not doe this feate for the
Duke then?

EUBELLA

I dare not.

HIPPOLITO

You wonot y'are resolv'd for his sake, why then prethee doo't for mine, you told me once you lov'd me,
Ile take it as a courtesie.

EUBELLA

I never lov'd your vicious wayes;

HIPPOLITO

My wayes, they shanot trouble you, Ile take my owne
Course, meet him but to night for my sake and twine with him.

EUBELLA

Ile sooner meete with a disease, with death;
You are ignoble, do you urge it as
An argument of my respect to you
To sinne against my love?

HIPPOLITO

I shall do no good upon her—were I the Duke, you should
Find another usage.

EUBELLA
A tirant might do any thing.

[Enter **DUKE**

DUKE
How now is she moist and supple?
Will she stoope to the impression?

HIPPOLITO
I told you sir, I was not arm'd toth' purpose, you tooke me un provided, at the next bou't I may do
somewhat, ith meane time let me Counsell you, to let her feed high, shee'le never fall low enough else,
she must be dieted, if you let her pick her sallets, you may fast another Lent, and all our paines be not
worth an egge at Easter.

DUKE
Come cruell faire one; we may take the aire together.

HIPPOLITO
So so Im'e discharged, now to my guest.

[Exeunt.

SCENE III

Hippolito's Lodgings.

[Enter **CLARIANA**.

CLARIANA
Not yet returnd? I shall expect too long
He is a hansome Gentleman and witty
I must not alwayes walke in clouds, his friend
Must bring us more acquainted, I do love him.
Not yet? his businesse has much force upon him.

[Enter **MILENA**.

MILENA
Madam the doores are lock'd

CLARIANA
What should this meane? he knowes me not
I cannot feare betraying.

[Enter **BELLAMENTE**.

BELLAMENTE
Now for this Ladybird ha!

MILENA
Madam tis Bellamente.

CLARIANA
Cupid defend wench, ha!

BELLAMENTE
Sure tis a dreame.

CLARIANA
All is at stake, I must be confident, how does my servant?

BELLAMENTE
I am wondering.

CLARIANA
To see me here I warrant.

BELLAMENTE
Is not your name Clariana?

CLARIANA
Yes.

BELLAMENTE
Tis not sure
You are some other Lady without a name
Whom our friend made a prisoner to his Chamber,
And cause his businesse with the Duke detaines him
Sent me to kisse your hand and disingage you.

CLARIANA
Will you not know me then?

BELLAMENTE
Yes now I looke better on you, y'are Claria a
To whom Bellamente hath devoted all
His loving honest service, she that gave me
Vowes in exchange of mine, if my eyes be not
Unfaithfull and delude me.

CLARIANA
Come Ile take
Your wonder off.

BELLAMENTE
Take it all off together, I ha not done
My admiration, have I not mistooke
My way and falne upon some other lodging?
Is this your dwelling Madam?

CLARIANA
No?

BELLAMENTE
His name, I pray you call the owner.

CLARIANA
Tis

BELLAMENTE
Tis so and I am miserable, false Clariana
O whither is the faith of women fled!

CLARIANA
Youle heare me sir?

BELLAMENTE
Was't not Hippolito,
Whom I so often did entreate to see her
My friend Hippolito, he wod not go with me
To her, that were too publicke, he had plots
And private meetings, Lady he has seene you now
And knowes you too,
And how dee like him Lady, does he not careere handsomely
In the Divells sadle? my soules upon a torture.

CLARIANA
Youle heare me sir?

BELLAMENTE
I must be mad come tell me, why do not I kill thee now.

CLARIANA
Tis in your power to be a murderer, but if you knew.

BELLAMENTE
I know too much but Ile begin with him.

CLARIANA
What dee meane?

BELLAMENTE

To write upon his hart he has abus'd me,
I like a tame foole must extoll his friendship
But never for his sake will I trust man
Nor woman, you have forfeited your soules
There's not a graine of faith nor honesty
In all your sexe, you have tongues like the Hyena
And onely speake us faire to ruine us
You carry springs within your eies and can
Out weepe the Crocadile, till our too much pitty
Betray us to your mercilesse devouring.

CLARIANA

When you are temperate enough to heare
The cause that brought me hither happily
You will repent this passion, in which
I must be bold to tell you sir, my honor
Suffers unkindly—and your friends.

BELLAMENTE

Grow not from fraile to impudent.

CLARIANA

You are resolved
To be impatient? when you are collected.

[Going.

BELLAMENTE

Stay I will heare, indeed I will, say any thing.

CLARIANA

First then you have no cause to accuse Hippolito
For breach of friendship, had he purpos'd any
Dishonor to your selfe through me, he could not
Be such a foole to send you to his chamber
Whoe's knowledge, it should last of all the world
Arrive at, if you soberly consider.
He knowes not so much of me, as my name;
Thinke then but with what justice, you have all
This while inveighed against him—for my selfe
I confesse freely sir I made a visit
But innocently and pure from any thought
To iniure you; I had a curiosity
To see the man you had so much commended
That was my fault, and I before you came
Accusd my selfe, and could without your furie.
Have chid my modesty enough. Yet sir

You tooke me in no action of dishonour
My maide was all my company.

BELLAMENTE
But you look'd for
One to returne, misfortune kept him from you
Tell me but this, if thou hast any truth
Could any woman Clariana, that
Would ha the world but thinke her virtuous
Suffer her selfe to be'lock'd up suspitiously
Within a strangers lodging.

CLARIANA
By all goodnesse
It was without my knowledge, I was weary
Expecting him, and meaning to depart;
Some minutes ere you came my servant told me
I was a prisoner, you have all the story
Which cannot, if but weighd with reason
Carry a crime like yours.

BELLAMENTE
Like mine?

CLARIANA
I ha said it
Tis you have made a greater fault then I,
With so much violence to condemne before
You know the offence, and I must tell you sir
But that my love is grounded upon virtue,
This were enough to stagger my affection
Raile at your Mistresse but for going abroad
To see your friend? so just a one? I see
You will be jealous when we are married.

BELLAMENTE
Never, you have awakd my honour Lady
I dare beleeve and aske thy pardon, trust me
I will command my passions hereafter
And if thou but consent, give proofe, all jealousie
Is flowne away, wee'le marry instantly
Should he retaine a thought not square of her
This will correct all, he is here, no word
Of discontent, put all off merrily.
Lets kiss.

[Kisses her.

[Enter **HIPPOLITO**.

HIPPOLITO
How now, he wo'not serve me so?

BELLAMENTE
We are acquainted and now you have seene
My Mistresse, I shall hope, we may enioy
Your company hereafter.

HIPPOLITO
Ha, your Mistresse?

BELLAMENTE
Mine, Clariana.

CLARIANA
Tis my name.

BELLAMENTE
Come sh'as told me all
Ile take her word nothing has past offensive,
Salute her now as mine, the character
I gave her, and thy resolution
Not to see her, engaged her to this travel.

HIPPOLITO
May I be confident, you have forgiven
My wilde discourse, my studies shall hereafter
bend all to serve you nobly.

CLARIANA
There is cause that I should beg your pardon.

BELLAMENTE
Weele not part.
Now till the Priest hath made all perfect.

HIPPOLITO
Ile assist the Clarke.

CLARIANA
You have power to steere me.

BELLAMENTE
Hymen light up thy Torches, woods of Pine
Should be cut up to make thy altars shine.

[Exeunt.

ACTUS TERTIUS

SCENE I

A Tavern.

Enter **SEBASTIAN**, **BONALDO**, and **DRAWER**.

SEBASTIAN
We might with more discretion have sent for wine
To my owne lodgings.

BONALDO
Ever while you live drinke wine at the fountaine.

SEBASTIAN [To the **DRAWER**]
Here I am not knowne, let no body interrupt us.

BONALDO
Let it be rich and sparckling, my precious varlet, and how
And how go things at Court?

[Exit **DRAWER**.

SEBASTIAN
After a cup or two Ile tell thee.

BONALDO
I would Hippolito were here, hee's a good fellow, and takes
After his father, the Duke makes much on him.

[Re-enter **DRAWER** with wine. Exit.

SEBASTIAN
Her'es a good health to him.

[Drinks.

BONALDO
Let it come, I am glad to see you sociable, come to the
City and leave purchasing, dirty acres.

SEBASTIAN
The same justice that mine had.

BONALDO
And it were as deepe as an vsurers conscience,
My boy should ha't.

[Enter **FIDLER**.

FIDLER
Wilt please you Gentlemen to heare any musicke.

BONALDO
Shall have any?

SEBASTIAN
By no meanes, it takes from our owne mirth.

BONALDO
Be gon then.

FIDLER
A very good song, and please you.

BONALDO
Yet agen, will you have your occupation broke about.
Your head?

FIDLER
Ile make you laugh Gentlemen.

BONALDO
Ile make you cry and tune your voyce to the lamentation
Of oh my fiddle, if you remove not presently.

[Exit **FIDLER**.

SEBASTIAN
This is the tricke of Tavernes, when men desire to be private.

BONALDO
Come whom shal we now remember? heres to your Mistresse.

[Drinks.

SEBASTIAN
A Mistresse at my yeeres?

BONALDO

Till threescore y'are allowd, I never wore more favours at one and twenty, this Riband came from a Countesse, this locke I weare for a young Ladies sake, this touch was the fall of a Gentlewomans fanne that is new come to Court.

SEBASTIAN
New come to Court? Ile pray for her, is she vertuous?

BONALDO
And she be, there is hope the Courtiers may convert her, here's
To her first.

[Enter **JUGLER**.

JUGLER
Gentlemen will you see a Iackanapes?

BONALDO
How many is there of you?

SEBASTIAN
Yet more o'these raskalls?

JUGLER
I can shew you very fine tricks.

BONALDO
Prethee Hocus Pocus, keepe thy grannams huckle bone.
And leave us.

SEBASTIAN
Presto be gon, or ile teach you a tricke for your Iackanapes
Learning, they will be deceiued that choose a Tauerne for privacie.

[Exit **JUGLER**.

BONALDO
Come our blood cooles; here's to your faire daughter.

SEBASTIAN
Poore girle, I thanke you sir.

BONALDO
I do not flatter you, but you may be proud, I say no more.

SEBASTIAN
Of what?

BONALDO

Your daughter, shee's a hansome Gentlewoman, the're be
Worse faces at Court.

SEBASTIAN
Her complexion is naturall, she has no tricke of art
A litle breeding she has had; and some precepts to guard her Honesty.

BONALDO
Honesty where is it?

SEBASTIAN
It should be every where

BONALDO
Take heed what you say, least you be made to justifie it
Honesty every where?
Heres to you, come.

[Drinks.

SEBASTIAN
I speake Bonaldo what I thinke, and it would be no
Dishonour to the greatest to be the first examples.

BONALDO
If all were of your mind who should thrive in this world?
Pledge me.
How shall Christians behave themselves in great offices?
Or under-clarkes purchase honesty? but one terme were enough to undoe the City, the Court were but in ill case if great men should stand upon't, for the Countrey, tis bought and sold every market day.
Come begin to me.

SEBASTIAN
Name it

BONALDO
To the Duke.

[Drinks.

SEBASTIAN
The Duke, he does not love me.

BONALDO
How?

SEBASTIAN
No Bovaldo he does not.

BONALDO

He loves your daughter—

SEBASTIAN

Tis not Princely, Nay I shall dare to tell him so, but
To his health.

[Drinks.

BONALDO

Let it come, me thinkes he is a very fine Gentleman.

SEBASTIAN

I begin to be warme already.

BONALDO

And one that loves a wench as well—

SEBASTIAN

As ill thou wodst say?

BONALDO

As ill as I, let it be so, I were no good subiect to deny it
To his Highnesse.

SEBASTIAN

Thou knewest me a Gentleman.

BONALDO

Are you not so still?

SEBASTIAN

No I'me a Knight, a Lord I know not what,
I'me lost within a wildernesse of names
But I will be my selfe agen—the tother cup.

BONALDO

Tis welcome, shall we double our files?

SEBASTIAN

This skirmish will doe well.

BONALDO

Charge me home then.

SEBASTIAN

Now I could talke me thinkes.

I will not prostitute Eubella for
The wealth of his whole Dukedome, ther'es no honor
To a noble conscience, he is the greatest coward.
Dares not be honest.

BONALDO
Right, if a man dares not be honest he is a Coward
But he that dares be dishonest.

SEBASTIAN
Dares cut his fathers throat

BONALDO
A pretty fellow heres to you agen; shalls have a wench? now am I addicted to embrace any thing in the likenesse of a woman, oh for a Chamber-maide to wrestle withall; send for a brace of Basaliskes, thou hast no spirit no Masculine vertue, now could I o're runne the whole Countrey of the Amazons. Heres to a Penthesilia beare up my valiant Mirmidon and we will do such feates shall make the Troians wonder at our backes and bring Dame Hellen to us.

SEBASTIAN
I prethee leave this humor, tis not generous.

BONALDO
How not generous take heed what you say.

SEBASTIAN
I shanot eate my words.

BONALDO
Then drinke your drinke,
Now Troy burnesblew, wheras Hecuba?

SEBASTIAN
Thou art all for wenching.

BONALDO
Upon a condition I will drinke to thee.

No, no, thou wot not doe so much, and a man should die for a lift a'the leg: the Duke has a great minde to thy daughter, he is but mortall flesh and bloud, there be subjects that have as sound bodies no dispraise to his Excelency.

SEBASTIAN
Dee not feare to talke thus?

BONALDO
Feare? would any durst send to me such
A virgin Pinnace, rigd and gay with all flags.

SEBASTIAN
This is uncivilll, and I shall tell Bonaldo.

BONALDO
Nay nay, thou art so waspish, if a friend desired a curtesie, that is in fashion; because the Duke—

SEBASTIAN
Y'are too bold, and forget your selfe, I am
Ashamd of this converse; because the Duke?
Did his hand graspe the Scepters of the world
And would propound e'm all to buy the honor
Of my Eubella, I would scorne his salarie
And tell him he were poorer in his soule
Then he that feedes ith hospitall, I'me armd
And shall grow very angry with your humor
Which ere it nam'd my daughter carried wickednesse
Enough, but in her cause I am easily
Provok'd to teach that tongue repentance dares
Traduce her whitnesse, I allow a mirth
But do not love this madnesse, and if I
Might counsell you, there is a way to quench
These wild licencious flames, earnest of those
Our soules shall feele hereafter, we are both
In yeeres, and should looke out our winding sheet
Not women.

BONALDO
Boy!

[Enter **DRAWER**.

Ile pay the reckoning; Be honest and see what will
Come on't
Ile seeke out my sonne Hippolito.
Hee'e be ruld by me, here's a coile about a tassell Gentle!

[Exit.

SEBASTIAN
Hee's drunke already
That which has raisd me but to noble anger
Is his distraction, theres for your wine.

[Gives the **DRAWER** money.

Now to the wanton Duke, heaven let him see
His shame and know, great men that practise lust

Both kill their body and corrupt their dust,
Let him fret do what he can,
The world shall call, Sebastian honest man.

[Exit.

A Room in Bellamente's House.

[Enter **HIPPOLITO**.

HIPPOLITO
Had I but one thing that did touch on honor
My friendship, and is that diseased already
And languishing? was it for this I would not
See her that I might trespasse with more guilt
When she was married? are not other women
As faire and tempting? or am I hurried
By violence of my fate to love her best
That should be most a stranger? and does she
Meet my modest flame? nay must the tapers
Sacred to Hymen light us to our sinnes?
Lust was too early up in both, oh man
Oh woman! that our fires had kissd like lightning
Which doth no sooner blaze but is extinct, shee's here.

[Enter **CLARIANA** and **PAGE**.

CLARIANA
Where's your master?

PAGE
There he is Madam.

CLARIANA
Why do you walke so melancholy sir?

HIPPOLITO
I was collecting my selfe about some businesse
Must be dispach'd this morning, sirra pray
The groome make ready my horse.

CLARIANA
Not yet
You do not meane to leave me o'the suddaine?

I am alone, my husband is at Court,
Pray rob me not of all my company,
I shall not thinke upon his absence, with
So much sorrow if you make me happy
With your society.

HIPPOLITO
There's the Divell already, I cannot leave her
My boy may go howsoever.

[Exit **PAGE**.

CLARIANA
Oh Hippolito
If you have usd no charmes but simple courtship,
Perhaps you may condemne me in your thoughts
That I so soone (not studying the wayes
Of cunning to disguise my love, which other
Women have practis'd, and would well become
The modesty of a wife) declare my selfe
At your dispose, but I suspect you have
Some command more then Naturall, I have heard
There have beene too much witchcraft exercis'd
To make poore women dote.

HIPPOLITO
You are not serious
In what you say? I hope you do not take me
For such a juggler? if you thinke I practice.

CLARIANA
That looke acquits you, then at my nativity
Some powerfull starre raignd, I have heard Astrologers
Talke much of Venus.

HIPPOLITO
And of Mars when they are
in coniunction, they encline us mortalls
Strangly to love and ly with one another.

CLARIANA
I am ignorant
What influence we have from them, but I
Am sure, something has strangely wrought on me.

HIPPOLITO
As how Madam?

CLARIANA

Why to love, I know not home,
You know my meaning, but truth witnesse with me
When first I saw your person I gave up
My liberty, me thought I lov'd you strangely.

HIPPOLITO

I had desires too I could not justifie
But knowledge that you were my friends, for that time
All loose fires, but love that swaid you, then quenchd
And kept your thoughts longing, met with my heart
And scald it up for you, yet when I thinke on Bellemente.
Theres wrestlings in my blood.

CLARIANA

Iust when I thinke on him tis so with mine,
That love should be so equall, do'st not stirre you
Sometimes to thinke of former vowes? Nay I do dreame
Sometimes of being surprizd in thy deere armes
And then methinkes I weepe, and sigh and wake.
With my owne grones.

HIPPOLITO

I never dreame of that

CLARIANA

It is my foolish fancie, yet such feares
Should waking never trouble me, those lovers
That have not art to hide, and to secure
Their amorous thefts, deserve to be reveald.

HIPPOLITO

Sure there's no woman in the world but this
Could have such power against my friend, each sillable
Renewes her force upon me.

CLARIANA

I beseech you
Although a storme hath throwne me on your shore
Have not so litle charity to thinke
I should accept of safety on another,
It is not possible any but your selfe
Withall the Magicke of his tongue or fortunes
Could bribe me from Bellemente, if I fall
For too much loving you, your mercy may
Interpret fairely, by these teares.

[Enter **PAGE** and **GROOME**.

GROOME

Sir your horse is ready

HIPPOLITO

I shanot go yet, Lady if you please
Wee'l walke a turneith Garden.

[Exeunt.

GROOME

Harke you my small friend, without offence is not your
Master a —

PAGE

What

GROOME

I would have another word for a whooremaster.

PAGE

How my durty rubber of horse heeles.

GROOME

Nay I do not say he is, I do but aske, whether he be or no, Be not angry demilance, there be as good
gentlemen as he, that love a wench.

PAGE

Why is your Mistresse a wench?

GROOME

My Mistresse you didapper.

PAGE

I do not say she is, I do but aske whether she be or no, there be as hansome creatures none dispraisd,
that take mony for their warren, have I answerd you my bold Marchant of dung in a wheele barrow?

GROOME

How now lackalent is shreeds of Satten, I shall swing you with a horse-rod, you whippet.

PAGE

Go meddle with your masters Gelding, and cheate him in the provender to keepe you in perpetuall pots
of Ale, when you entertaine the Kitchinmaide in the hayloft, talke of my Master?

GROOME

Meddle with my Mistresse?

PAGE

Yes Ile speake to her to allow you a lesse proportion of cleane straw to rubb bootes and ly in sirra, you thinke you are at rack and manger, when you devide beanes with the horses and helpe to foule the stable.

GROOME
Sirra whelpe that has eaten knot-grasse, do not provoke me least I fetch a smith and curry your thin sids.

PAGE
Mine you beane-shifter, would you durst no better ride booty at the horse match or cosen your Master ith next parcell of Oates, I feare you not my canvas serving-man with halfe a livery, groome othe stable once removd from the farrier.

[Enter **HIPPOLITO**, **CLARIANA**.

CLARIANA
What at difference?
Both No not we Madam.

HIPPOLITO
Sirra come hither.
Entreat my father meet me at Court.

PAGE
I shall sir

HIPPOLITO
Theres no hast for my Nag yet.

[Exit.

CLARIANA
About your businesse sira.

GROOME
My businesse is below staires, and with a Gelding, what he may prove I know not well, what I thinke I will keepe to my selfe, my Lady may be honest enough, but he that is borne to be a Cuckold shall never dy a bachelor.

[Exit.

SCENE III

A Room in the Duke's Palace.

[Enter **DUKE**, **EUBELLA**.

[A Song which done, enter **SEBASTIAN** and **COURTIERS**.

DUKE
My Lord you are welcome.

SEBASTIAN
Give me leave to tell
Your highnesse I suspect it.
Why should a Prince dissemble?

DUKE
This dialect becomes you not.

SEBASTIAN
Sir sir I must be honest.

EUBELLA
Father.

SEBASTIAN
Eubella expresse thy duty
To him thou calst a father, for thy owne
Sake leave this place, the Court's afire.

DUKE
How sir?

SEBASTIAN
Canst thou not see the flames that threaten thee?

DUKE
Sebastian's wild.

SEBASTIAN
But you would make her tame, looke looke Eubella
The Duke himselfe burnes, do not his eyes sparcke
With lust, his very breath will blast thee.

EUBELLA
I feare this will be dangerous, good sir.

SEBASTIAN
If yet thou hast not lost thy innocence
I charge thee, by thy mothers memory
And colder ashes, keepe thy selfe unstaind
Let no temptation corrupt a thought
Th'art richer in thy chastity, then all
The Kings of earth can make thee, if thou fall

Thou kilst my heart.

DUKE
All this for thy sake we forbeare to punish,
But you should know my Lord.

SEBASTIAN
Lord me no Lords
I grone under the burden of your honors
And here resigne all, give me but my daughter.

DUKE
Let not your passion strangle thus your reason.

SEBASTIAN
Let not a sinne so blacke as lust degrade
A Prince and register thy dishonord name
With foule adulteries.

DUKE
You are very bold.

SEBASTIAN
I would preserve the name of our yet honest family;
I feare she is o'ercome already, I do not like her silence.

DUKE
To take off your feares
Although we neede not give you satisfaction,
By this white brow, she is as pure as when
She came to Court.

SEBASTIAN
Oh let Sebstian fall
Lower sir, I beseech you tread upon me
So you will still be honest to my child,
She is all my comfort.

DUKE
Rise.

SEBASTIAN
But will you not
Hereafter study to betray her innocence?
Or give her licence to returne with me?
Ile aske no more assurance, grant but this
And when we are at home, it shall oblige us
Beside the duties we already owe

In heart to pray for you.

DUKE
We are not pleasd, she should depart.

SEBASTIAN
Then Ile vnthanke your Goodnesse
And dare thus boldy tell your highnesse, lawes
Are most vnjust that punish petty theeves
And let the great ones scape.

DUKE
We are yet patient.

EUBELLA
Deere sir

SEBASTIAN
Princes may take our children from us, not
To aduance but kill their names, corrupt their vertues;
When needy men, that steale to feed their lives
Are doo'md to the Gallouse.

DUKE
Take the frantick hence.

SEBASTIAN
Take hence the ravisher.

COURTIER
Sebastian.

SEBASTIAN
Although he ravish not Eubella
From her selfe, yet he does ravish
A daughter from her father, and ile voice it
Through every streete, I am not bound to whisper
When griefes so loud within me.

DUKE
Place him where his noise may make his owne headake not others,
This liberty of tongue shall be corrected.

SEBASTIAN
It will but spread thy infamy, when men
Shall speake my cause, and thy lasciviousnes
Which I will tell so often to the stones
The vault shall be ashamd to eccho thee Eubella.

DUKE
Away with him.

SEBASTIAN
Do bury me alive, be strong Eubella
And let not death by my example shake thee.

DUKE
This may incline her, do not weepe Eubella
They are not worth a teare, yet tis within
Thy power to ransome their bold heads, were they
Humbled toth block, this Pitty shewes a child
But Princes loose their awe that are too mild.

[Exeunt.

SCENE IV

A Room in Bellamente's House.

[Enter **BELLAMENTE** and **SERVANT**

BELLAMENTE
Where's your Lady?

SERVANT
In her Chamber.

BELLAMENTE
Whoe's with her?

SERVANT
None but the Gentleman you left here.

BELLAMENTE
Hippolito? I wonot have so base a thought—Ilt to e'm,
Yet, you may go and say I am returnd and wish her presence.
Ha! there is something busie with my braine.

[Exit **SERVANT**.

And in the shape of jealousie presents
A thousand feares, they have beene very loving
Since we were married; thou soules corrupter
Who sent thee to me? to distract my peace,

Be gon, be gon, and scatter thy foule seedes
Vpon a ground that will be fruitfull to thee.
The innocence I carry in my breast
Armes me against the thoughts of others treason,
My friend, my wife? the very names are sacred
And like the heads of Saints, and holy Martyrs
Invested with such glorious beames they strike
Conspiracy blind, how now, whats in thy face?

[Enter **SERVANT**.

SERVANT.
Oh sir?

BELLAMENTE
Whats the matter?

SERVANT
Would you could understand without my tongue.

BELLAMENTE
How does thy Lady?

SERVANT
My Lady is—

BELLAMENTE
Ha! why dost pause vilaine? answer me.

SERVANT
Alas I know not with what words to tell you
Would I had never seene her, or you never
Married her.

BELLAMENTE
Ha! stay there, Shall I trust thee now fury? but speake, and
Be not tedious, what is my Lady doing upon thy life?

SERVANT
Alas sir it will make you madde.

BELLAMENTE
Speake or never speake agen, I am prepard.

SERVANT
Pardon my unhappinesse to deliver then
A truth that will distract you, you have now
Nor friend nor wife.

BELLAMENTE
Are they both dead?

SERVANT
Yes dead to honor, finding her chamber lockt
I know not what did prompt me to make use
Of a small cranny, where I beheld em both,
I want modest language
To tell how they are falne, and yet too soone
I know you cannot choose but understand me.

BELLAMENTE
How long hast thou beene a Raven?

SERVANT
Good sir collect your selfe,
Tis my misfortune and no fault to be
The sad reporter.

BELLAMENTE
Do I live still?

SERVANT
And shall I hope long.

BELLAMENTE
Th'art most uncharitable, if thou hadst lou'd
Thy master thou wouldst wish him happinesse
Which all life denies, is my composition
So hard, a sorrow great and high like this
Cannot disolve it? wonot my heart breake
With this? then melt it some celestiall fire,
In pitty of my sufferings some cloud
Of raine, since my owne eyes refuse to drowne me,
Fall and orewhelme this miserable Island.

SERVANT
Sir,

BELLAMENTE
Can this be possible? be sure they are Divells
Or I shall find such a new hell for thee—

SERVANT
I would it were not true.

BELLAMENTE

Some mercifull whirlewind snatch this burden up
And carry it into some wildernesse:
Leave not
If it were possible the mention
Of what I was behind, the wolues are honester
Then mankind is to man, I prethee kill me
I kneele to be destroyd, it is thy duty;
When thou shalt tell the world my wretched story
And what soule killing and devouring griefes
Thy good hand rid me of, it shall acquit thee
And call thy murder charity.

SERVANT
Good sir.

BELLAMENTE
O whither shall I runne to find a friend
Will do the gentle office to despatch me
Without my owne hand?

SERVANT
Rather live to take
Iustice upon their periuries.

BELLAMENTE
Good man.
My better Angel how had I forgot
My selfe? Coward to thinke of dying yet.
Who would put confidence in heaven hereafter.
If it should suffer me depart the world.
Without revenge, and that my owne upon em.
Come draw, take my sword, I will be double arm'd▪
I charge thee by thy duty, or thy life
If that be more, stay you at bottome of
The staires, while I ascend their sinfull chamber
And if my Pistoll misse his treacherous heart
He has no way to passe but on thy sword,
The place gives such advantage that with
Safety thou maist command his life.
Kill him with losse compunction then a witch
Fleas a dead Infant for his skin to perfect
A hellish incantation, thou wo't do't?

SERVANT
Ile do my best he shall not 'scape.

BELLAMENTE
Wife, friend,

You hang like vlcers on me, I am bound
To cut you from my heart to cure my wound.

[Exeunt.

SCENE I

Clariana's Chamber.

Enter **HIPPOLITO** and **CLARIANA** upon a bed.

HIPPOLITO
What pitty tis these pleasures are not lawfull.

CLARIANA
Lawfull? that would take much from the delight
And value, I have heard some Gentlemen,
That want no venison of their owne,
Sweare they had rather strike their neighbors deere
Then hunt in their owne parke, what we possesse
We keepe for our necessity, not game,
Or wearied with enjoying give't a way
To purchase thanks abroad.

HIPPOLITO
For all that Madam, there is danger in some purlies, and when the Keeper is none of the wisest, their bolts are sooner shot, I like the sport, but would not be taken at the deere stealing, yet for such a Doe as thou art, I would venter—

CLARIANA
Tis no glory to take a towne without some hazard, that victorie is sweetest which is got in the face of danger, when the very cannons are hoarse with clamor, then the bold souldier goes on and thinkes the noise loude musicke to him, give me the man that feares no colours, was there ever any thing worth the enioying that came easily and without trouble to us? what makes a maidenhead the richer purchase thinke you? but I am married and my husband is your friend.

HIPPOLITO
Prethee no more o'that.

CLARIANA
No more othat, in my conscience you are fearefull this is the ballad right. Courtier hey Courtier ho, wilt thou be my true love, no no no, fy upon't. I should name my husband often to arme and fortifie our selves▪ I confesse, I do not wish him here, perhaps he would do some mischiefe, and hinder another meeting, but if he were present now, and should see us kisse, for and he' were ten husbands, I would

trust his eyes no further, what could he say? for he did but kisse her, for he did but kisse her, and so let her go: come for shame be more sprightly, I have as much reason to looke about, and play my game wisely, if my Cards were considerd.

HIPPOLITO
Yet you are very confident.

CLARIANA
He does use to keep his word, I know heele not returne this two houres, come we are secure, prethee lets talke o something els.

[Enter **BELLAMENTE**.

BELLAMENTE
Of death.
Are ye untwin'd?

CLARIANA
Are we betray'd.

BELLAMENTE
You did not looke for me—your sword is of no use, dee see.

[Presenting a pistol at **HIPPOLITO**.

Pitty your owne damnations; and obey me, get into that closet no considering, it must be done.

[Shuts **HIPPOLITO** in the closet.

So you are fast, now Lady Lechery dresse you the bed a litle, and lay the pillowes hansomely bestirre you.

CLARIANA
Vpon my knees—

BELLAMENTE
No petitioning, you can sing, quickly or—so so, you sirra at the bottome of the staires, come up. Be wise and do not kneele nor whimper.

[Enter **SERVANT**.

Now sirra speake and tell me truly
Or ile search every corner of thy soule
Why didst thou play the vilaine, thus to mocke me
With expectation to find my wife
Playing the adulteresse with Hippolito?
Tell me?

SERVANT

Hold sir I beseech you.

BELLAMENTE

What Divell did instruct thee to disquiet
My heart, secure and confident of their honors
As conscious of my owne, no head but mine
To bruise with jealosie, where is he? shew me
Or take into thy bosome what my vowes
Had fixt for him and her.

[Presents the pistol at him.

SERVANT

If these be eyes I saw em'.

BELLAMENTE

If these be eyes, is that your proofe, lay such
A cause upon the strength of a weake sence
That is a thousand wayes deceiv'd, your eyes!
O Clariana, this impudent slave
With such a cunning face, told me thou wert
Naught, lock'd in the lustfull armes of base
Hippolito, my friend, my honest friend.
One that commands not his owne life so much
As I, that wo'd not for a Monarchy
Do me the least disgrace, hast found him vilaine?

SERVANT

Ile looke under the bed sir.

BELLAMENTE

And I beleevd him too, and had I found
But the least point of such a sinne, within
Thy Chamber, furies should appeare more tame
then Bellamente, hell should not have malice.
Enough to adde to my revenge, but pardon.
My easie credulous nature, I confesse.
A fault, for had I lov'd thee nobly as
Became our holy vowes, our vowes Clariana
To which we cald the Angells, I should never
Have entertained one thought against thy chastity
But this slave shall repent it.

SERVANT

Hold, I beseech you sir? by my life I thought
I saw em.

BELLAMENTE
Thought? is that excuse?

SERVANT
Good sir, Ile never trust my owne eyes after this
There was deceptio visus. Oh be mercifull!

BELLAMENTE
None but her honor, and my friends to poison?
Had this report not first arrived at me
How had we all beene shamd—dost thou kneele too
[To **CLARIANA**] Nay then I must forgive him, rise my honest
My deerest Clariana—but I shall heare
You will be prating of it, if one sillable
Come to my eare let fall by thee, that touches
But thy suspition, Ile ha thy tongue
And heart.

SERVANT
Cut me into a thousand peeces. Madam your pardon
How was I cozen'd!

BELLAMENTE
Be gon and thanke her goodnesse thou dost live
But do not dare to be so desperate
To come within my eye reach till I call thee.

SERVANT
Ile not come neere you, Ile bury my selfe in the Cellar.

[Exit.

BELLAMENTE
So so. Now sir you may come forth agen
Nor do you my most excellent whoore, thinke
There is no storme to follow—keepe your distance
You have had a feast, a merry one, the shot
Is now to be discharg'd, what do you expect?

HIPPOLITO
Death, from that hand, I apprehend no mercie
Not have I so much innocenee to hope
You will delay your justice,, were I arm'd
With power to resist, I should adde more
Offences by defending of this life
That has so basely iniured you.

BELLAMENTE

Treacherous serpent

HIPPOLITO
With this I have sometime releeud your valour
And had no pitty of my blood, but then
I was a friend, in such a cause as this
I have no arme no weapon, not, if I
Were sure the bullet would dceline my heart.
It does beget a cowardise to thinke
How I am falne.

CLARIANA
O pardon

BELLAMENTE
Pardon with what conscience canst thou aske it?

HIPPOLITO
You shewed a charity above my hope
By giving a few minutes for my prayer,
Which shewes you had no meaning to destroy
The soule, twas Rare compassion, but if you
Could possibly forgive?

BELLAMENTE
How forgive

HIPPOLITO
I say if it were possible you could
Remitt so foule (in me the blakst) offence
Not for the love I have to number dayes
But by some noble service, to wash off
This shame, this leprosie upon my name.

BELLAMENTE
Ha you found it now.

HIPPOLITO
I have but vainely interrupt your fury
You cannot must not pardon it, such mercie
Becomes not an Italian.

BELLAMENTE
Miserable woman.

CLARIANA
O sir, it was my first offence, what woman is
Without some staine? if all that in this kind

Have sinn'd, had met with present death you would
Not find some names, that now shine gloriously
Within the catalogue of Saints, my soule
Is full of shame and teares.

BELLAMENTE
Tell me Clariana.
Still I shall hit upon thy name, how couldst thou
Vse me so cruelly? did I want youth
And spring about me were my embraces cold
Frost in my blood? or in thy bed was I
Conueyd a snowball, rould up the children
Do to play with winter, did I not affect thee
Beyond all the comfort of the world?

CLARIANA
I know it.

BELLAMENTE
And thou whom best of all mankind I lov'd
Whose friendship tooke up my whole heart till she
Came in a wife, yet then thou hadst a seate
One small degree below her, when this shall be
The talke of Ferrara who shall trust his friend
For thy sake, or at the mention of thy name
For sweare ever to marry?

CLARIANA
Noble sir.
It is within your power.

BELLAMENTE
To kill you both.

HIPPOLITO
I am prepared so well.
As this short time will give me leave.

CLARIANA
Tis yet within your power to silence all,
What is already done should we turne fountaines
We heartily may grieve for, not repaire,
The world can have no knowledge of our trespasse
Nor your dishonor, If you call it so
Vnlesse you tell it, you have nobly sir
Secur'd all shame at home, which has won more
Repentance from me then my teares, go on
Increase that piety, and be not you

The trumpet of their infamy abroad
Whose lives hereafter may be spent with such
Religious sorrow for offending you
That you may not repent to have forgiven.

BELLAMENTE
Shall I be wonne with foolish pitty?

CLARIANA
Our death will gaine you nothing, but the feare
You shannot keepe your owne life.

HIPPOLITO
Or if bloud
Must onely satisfie, let your sword here
Bath in revenge, the greatest sinner kill
If men were not, what woman could be ill.

BELLAMENTE
Your feares thus vanish, I delight not in
The bloody sacrifie, live both.

HIPPOLITO
A miracle.

CLARIANA
But ile do more then kill you—tak my love off.
I do desire never to see you more,
Nor will I be a Courtier to occasion
Meeting hereafter, what is done is circled
Within our knowledge, pray, farwell, for you
I do desire never to bed thee more
Ile force some smiles to keepe suspition off
But feare I never shall love heartily
Agen, thou hast undone me here, Clariana
And yet I wonot wish thee dead for this
Repent and when I die aske for a kisse.

[Exeunt.

SCENE II

A Room in the Palace.

[Enter **BONALDO** and a **COURTIER**.

BONALDO

Not at the Court? why he desired I should meet him here.

COURTIER

The Duke hath often asked for him.

BONALDO

He waites well in the meane time, who in the name of wantonnesse keepes him away, I know tis a wench, tis a parlous boy, my owne sonne to a haire, and he should not love a woman I would disinherit him, for I am of opinion an Athist sometime is better then an Eunnch, And yet cannot the Court find him game enough, but he must leape the pale and straggle so farre for Venison, that the Duke must hunt after him; and he were not my owne flesh and bloud, I would counsell him to marry, but they are dangerous, and a disease is more curable then a wife, for she indeed is a hectick feaver although I buried mine seven yeere agoe, yet I feele a grudging of her still, and for a need could guesse at the change of weather by the knowledge her noise has infused into my bones.

[Enter **DUKE**, **COURTIERS**.

COURTIER

The Duke.

DUKE

Some one looke out Hippolito.

BONALDO

If please your grace let it be my imployment.

DUKE

Signior Bonaldo?

BONALDO

Your highnesse humble servant. I am sorry my sonne should be absent, when your grace has service for him, but Ile find him out, I am acquainted with two or three of his haunts I know a Taverne is next doore to a—

DUKE

To a what?

BONALDO

It has a course name.

DUKE

No matter.

BONALDO

To a baudyhouse.

DUKE

Thats not impossible.

BONALDO
To find him there, I cannot helpe it?

COURTIER
He loves him the better for't.

BONALDO
Tis a tricke he learnd in France sir, where your nobility practise, he will leave it, when Capring and Kissing are out of fashion with Gentlemen.

DUKE
Oh he is young, I have heard you were as wild at his Yeeres.

BONALDO
And wilder too I should be sorry else.

DUKE
How?

BONALDO
I had ne're broke my wives heart else, with supping abroad and midnight revells▪ I should ha beene troubled with her till this time.

DUKE
She was a shrew it seemes? but you promise actively still?

BONALDO
Not much for the crosse point,
But with your highnesse licence, Ile find out Hippolito
To attend your pleasure.

DUKE
Good Signior.

[Exit.

A blunt honest Gentleman.

COURTIER
He does not boast much honesty, with your pardon sir.

DUKE
I like the freedome of his discourse, but see Hippolito

[Enter **HIPPOLITO**.

HIPPOLITO
I must not appeare melancholy.

COURTIER
Signior the Duke expects you.

HIPPOLITO
His graces humble creature.

COURTIER
Now is he come from some vaulting schoole Ile lay my life,
He is a pretty Gentleman tis pitty that nothing can perswade him from the flesh.

2ND COURTIER
The Duke imployes him.

COURTIER
I leiger at home.

HIPPOLITO
Both in prison!

DUKE
Both.
We all know Eubella, her father is committed to prison for being
To free on's tongne.

HIPPOLITO
Be confident I will prevaile, I have a new spell for her.

DUKE
Be speedy and be fortunate, she is in that chamber
Returne with her consent to love and be
What the Dukes power can make thee.

HIPPOLITO
You too much honor me.

DUKE
Come Gentleman.

[Exeunt **DUKE** and **COURTIERS**.

[**HIPPOLITO** seemes to open a chamber doore and brings forth **EUBELLA**.

HIPPOLITO
Lady, I am sent to know your full and finall resolution touching the businesse the Duke propounded,
though your father be shut up yet change of aire is fitter for your complexion, the Duke is a Gentleman

that may command in these parts tis not for want of provision, the Duke has a mind to cut up your virginity.

EUBELLA
If this be your affaire sir, tell the Duke
Eubella is a rocke.

HIPPOLITO
Thats very hard.

EUBELLA
His mermaids cannot winne me with their songs
Nor all his tempests shake me.

HIPPOLITO
Stay a litle
There's something more in my commission.

EUBELLA
Hippolito
I now have argument to thinke you were
Not borne a Gentleman, something, here is witnesse
I pittie thee, this is no noble office.

HIPPOLITO
You meane a pander it ha's been a thriving way for some,
But I am imployed by his grace.

EUBELLA
Shall feare or flattery
Corrupt a generous soule? I am a woman
The weakest of a thousand yet I dare
Give man example, rather to be sacrificed.
Then betray vertues cause, we give our life
To grow agen, from our owne funerall pile
Like the Assyrian brid.

HIPPOLITO
Thou hast so rich
A stocke of goodnesse, were all other women
Vitious, thou mightst impart enough to make
The whole sexe white agen, and leave thy selfe
One degree lesse then angell: canst thou pardon
That I have tempted thee so farre? thy hand
To give it a relligious kisse, when next
My tongue is orator in so foule a cause
The argument it selfe turne a disease
And eate it to the roote. I am chang'd Eubella

And more to trie thy strength then to orecome
I speake nowe for the Duke, keepe still thy thoughts
Deuout to honor, after I have studied
A yeares repentance for my wrongs to thee,
I will presume to say I love Eubella.

EUBELLA
But hath Hippolito no other meaning?
I understand, and take some joy to heare this language.

HIPPOLITO
The first proofe of my conversion
Shall be to tell the Duke he has done ill
To court thee sinfully.

[Enter **DUKE** and **COURTIERS**.

DUKE
Howes this?

EUBELLA
Pray do not mocke, if you knew how much,
Delight heaven takes to heare you speake so well
To the distressed Eubella.

HIPPOLITO
By this lip
If my profane touch make thee not offended
There is no good I will not act, nor ill
I will not suffer to deserue thy love
But I am miserable and cannot merit
I have not beene at home these many yeeres
Yet I will call my conscience to account
For all, and throw my selfe upon heavens charity,
Why dost thou weepe?

EUBELLA
My ioy can weare no other livery
Then teares, and confident all this is truth
I cannot keepe it in, you shall dispose
Eubellas heart.

HIPPOLITO
Then here I take it in
To my possession.

DUKE
Vilaine Strumpet.

HIPPOLITO
Sir, here are none such I can assure your highnesse.

DUKE
Is this your faith to me?

HIPPOLITO
I never did you.
True service till this minute, and I dare
Now tell you, though you cut my head off, tis
Not justice to pursue the ruine of
A harmelesse maid.

DUKE
Traytor

HIPPOLITO
Call me some Name, I understand my Lord
This virgin now is mine.

DUKE
Your whoore.

HIPPOLITO
This cannot make me yet forget your person.

EUBELLA
Sir I beseech you.

DUKE
By my Dukedome.

HIPPOLITO
The more you vex the more we grow together
In honor and chast love.

DUKE
You speake as if
You were to be her husband.

HIPPOLITO
Tis a title a prince should be ambitious of.

DUKE
Very fine
Do you consent too, to be cald his wife?

EUBELLA
If he dare make me such there is no second
My heart affects.

DUKE
Ist come to this? then heare what I determine.

EUBELLA
Sir consider

DUKE
I have considered do not interrupt me
Too morrow if I live Ile see you both
Married, thou excellent maide forgive my passion,
Accept him freely, thou hast overcome
With chastity, and taught me to be a prince
Which character, my lust had neere defac'd
Release Sebastian.

[Exit a **COURTIER**.

EUBELLA
What dutie can poore Eubella pay?

DUKE
No more, good deeds reward themselves, how have we slept.

HIPPOLITO
This exceeds all your favours.

DUKE
Cherish my gift Hippolito, she is a wife for the best prince, no honor can be enough to satisfie thy vertue.

[Exit,

COURTIER
Heres a strange whirle, I do not like it, if the Duke continue this mind, we must all be honest.

2ND COURTIER
Who can helpe it?

SCENE III

A Room in Bellamente's House.

[Enter **BELLAMENTE** and **BONALDO** at severall doores.

BONALDO
Save you Signior is my sonne here?

BELLAMENTE
He wa's here very lately, too late.

BONALDO
You do not answer as you were wont,
I aske for Hippolito, your friend.

BELLAMENTE
And did not I answer you?
Cry you mercie Signior, indeed he is not here.

BONALDO
How is it with your beauteous Clariana?

BELLAMENTE
Shee's well.

BONALDO
Pray commend my service to her.

BELLAMENTE
What said yee?

BONALDO
Nothing but my service to your Lady.

BELLAMENTE
Oh I thanke you, pray stay, and tell me how I looke.

BONALDO
Looke?

BELLAMENTE
They will perswade me within I am not well
I must confesse there is some cause of melancholy
Within me.

BONALDO
I guest so at first sight, may I presume to aske it?

BELLAMENTE
And yet does not concerne me in a higher nature then
My friend, a scuruy chance late hapn'ed to him
One that he lov'd most deerely, you will scarce

Beleeve, made him a Cuckold.

BONALDO
That all?

BELLAMENTE
That all. Dee understand what I have said?

BONALDO
Yes a friend was made a Cuckold by a friend
He did his wife and him a curtesie.

BELLAMENTE
Go home and pray, y'are in a desperate state
This is enough to weigh thee downe to hell.

BONALDO
I am not of your mind, and I had don't my selfe, I should
Never had so much despaire as to hang my selfe, why tis as
Common as shifting a trencher.

BELLAMENTE
But harke you sir, how ere you talkeou cannot in your judgement thinke so, are you married?

BONALDO
What dee see in my forehead you should thinke me so miserable?

BELLAMENTE
Ile tell you then, what a wife is, or should be.

BONALDO
I can tell you, what they should be.

BELLAMENTE
What?

BONALDO
They should be honest and love their husbands, and for their Sakes their bastards, which if they
understand they are bound, to keepe, because their ill conditions drive us a broad to get 'em.

BELLAMENTE
No, heare me.
A wife is mans best peece, who till he marries
Wants making up, she is the shrine to which
Nature doth send us forth on Pilgrimage,
She was a syens taken from that tree
Into which if she have no second grafting
The world can have no fruit, she is mans

Arithemeticke which teaches him to number
And multiply himselfe in his owne children,
She is the good mans Paradise, and the bads
First step to heaven, a treasure which who wants
Cannot be trusted to posterity
Nor pay his owne debts, she is a golden sentence
Writ by our maker, which the Angells may
Discourse of, only men know how to use
And none but devills violate.

BONALDO
All this youle justifie a wife.

BELLAMENTE
Now tell me Signior what punishment
That man deserves, that should deface or steale
This wealth away.

BONALDO
How meane you in the way of lying with her?
I am of my first opinion, there is not much treason
In't, if she be hansome.

BELLAMENTE
But is there no respect of friendship to be observ'd?

BONALDO
Nor kindred much in such a case.

BELLAMENTE
Would you not chide your sonne that should abuse his
Deere friends wife or Mistresse?

BONALDO
Yes if he should abuse her, but if he did but ly with her I should commend him, make the case your owne
would you deny a friend that wanted linnen the curtesie of your cleane shirt? a woman is a more
necessary wearing, and yet never the worse for't.

BELLAMENTE
Away thou wot infect my dwelling else,
To what a monster, is man growne.

BONALDO
Fare you well sir, I ha but answered to your questions.

BELLAMENTE
Cynick Ile hold thy Lanthorne now, and goe with thee
Through Athens and the world to find one man

That's honest.

[Enter **HIPPOLITO'S PAGE**.

PAGE
My Master remembers his humble service.

BELLAMENTE
To me? Ide rather thanke him to forget it
Why does he trouble me with letters? yet Ile read em.
Ha! to be married to morrow—This is an honest
Sentence, my heart bleeds still for wronging you.

[Enter **CLARIANA**.

Clariana Tis no secret.

[Gives her the letter.

CLARIANA
Ha to Eubella, I shanot conceale my passion, he must not marry.

BELLAMENTE
Give me the paper.

CLARIANA
Inspire me love ile crosse it

[Exit.

BELLAMENTE
Why does thy master boy, send me this letter?

PAGE
I know not sir; unlesse it be to certifie you of his marriage?

BELLAMENTE
He will marry now and live honest, heaven give him joy.
But its not so faire to disturbe my braine
That is not fully setled with his triumphes,
What ist to me? He cannot satisfie.
My jniurie if he should court his wife
And prevaile with her
To imbrace me too.
The Duke he writes, will honor his solemnity
His conscience dares not suffer him to invite
Me as his guest, why then must I be troubled
Cannot he laugh and hum and kisse his bride

But he must send me word, whose soule he has
Put miserably out of tune.

[Re-enter **CLARIANA** with a letter.

CLARIANA
Conceale that letter from all eyes but your Masters.

BELLAMENTE
Sirra you shall returne, and say I will dy shortly.

PAGE
Heaven forbid sir.

BELLAMENTE
That is a kind of prayer, who bad thee thee sayo?
Then if I must live, Ile find out a Hermit
That dwells within the earth or hollow tree.
A great way hence there I shall be secure
And learne to pray for I want charity—be gon boy.

CLARIANA
Good sir talke not so strangely.

BELLAMENTE
Fare you well too, Ile come agen to morrow, or I know
Not when, I have much businesse abroad.

CLARIANA
Will you ride forth?

BELLAMENTE
Yes.

CLARIANA
Shall none attend you?

BELLAMENTE
No I shall be best alone, you know your chamber
Theres none so bold to rob me of my griefe
Yet he thats sad as I; beares his owne thiefe.

ACTUS QUINTUS

SCENE I

Hippolito's Lodgings.

[Enter **HIPPOLITO** and his **PAGE**.

HIPPOLITO
I Know not what to resolue, this letter has distracted me It is not wisedome to acquaint Eubella, let me perus't agen. Sir, though I have repented my love, which drew my dishonor, I have not lost my charitie, and therefore can take no pleasure in your ruine, meet me to morrow earely in the groue behind the Pallace, I will discover a plot against your life, I pitty your danger, and will secure more ioyes to your bride, be secret yet and trust her, that is no otherwise then nobly yours, Clariana.

CLARIANA
Tis some thing Bellamente has designd.
For his revenge, did he speake strangely saist?

PAGE
Very strangely sir, he said he would dy shortly

HIPPOLITO
Thou didst mistake him, he meant I should dy, he will not kill me at the altar? perhaps I shall be poisoned at dinner, a thousand wayes there are to let out life—I must be certaine. Eubella and her father!

[Enter **EUBELLA** and **SEBASTIAN**.

Some truce with my affliction.

SEBASTIAN
More welcome then my liberty, Eubella
Has made my heart glad with your new character
And now my sonne Hippolito.

HIPPOLITO
That title
Will be aboue all honors the Duke can
Let fall upon me, that I have beene wild
I must with shame remember, but my study
Of after life to her and all the world
I hope shall purchase thee a better name.

SEBASTIAN
You will not leave us this morning?

HIPPOLITO
I shall returne, excuse me a few minutes.

EUBELLA
Do what you please; but if it be a businesse

You may dispence with—

HIPPOLITO
It concernes my honor, but nothing shall
Detaine me long; all places are but darkenesse
Without thy eies, Ile visit em' agen.

EUBELLA
How soone?

HIPPOLITO
You shall scarce thinke me absent

SEBASTIAN
We must expect you then.

HIPPOLITO
May the day shine bright upon thee.

EUBELLA
And all the blessings of it waite on you!

[Exit **HIPPOLITO**.

[Enter **BONALDO**.

SEBASTIAN
Signior you are most welcome, I entreat you
To call my girle your daughter.

BONALDO
My sonne has made this choise I heare, Ile
Call her any thing.

EUBELLA
I shall expresse my duty sir, in all things.

BONALDO
But wheres Hippolito—a buxome thing.

SEBASTIAN
Sir please you retire, he is new departed.

BONALDO
Whither? a musical lip.

SEBASTIAN
Nay we did not examine his affaire

But we expect his quicke returne.

EUBELLA
Wilt please you sir.

BONALDO
I should be pleasd with such another,—a light wench
And a yare, Ile attend you Lady.

[Exit.

SCENE II

A Room in Bellamente's House.

[Enter **CLARIANA, MILENA**.

CLARIANA
Be just Milena to me, and endeere
My love for ever.

MILENA
Madam you know my faith.

CLARIANA
I promist to meet
Hippolito this morning in the grove
Behind the Pallace, to conferre about
Some businesse that concernes, thou shat presently
Excuse my travell and intreate him hither,
He and my husband lately had some difference
I know not why, in this convenient absence
Of Bellamente he securely may
Speake with me here, yet Ile not willingly
Have him come hither by the publick way,
The Garden doore shall be left open for him
And a cleare passage to this Chamber.

MILENA
Madam I understand.

CLARIANA
Prevaile with him to come, tell him all's safe.

MILENA
Ile sweare it Madam to do you service.

CLARIANA

But use all hast.
Which way shall I beginne, I shall want art
I feare to winne upon him, oh for some
High, and prevailing oratory to
Expresse what my heart labours with! I could
Accuse my unkind desteny, declame
Against the power of love, raile at the charmes
Of language and proportion, that betray us
To hasty sorrow, and too late repentance,
But breath is this way lost, wounds that are made
Require a balsome, and not empty curses
To state our body, should the Marriner
When a storme meetes him, throw away his Card
Neglect himselfe and vessell; and ly downe
Cursing the winds and tempest? If he come
As but to doubt doth make me miserable
The genius of love assist my passion,
I must deliver something that doth make
My poore heart swell, and will if I conceale it
Like fire lockd up in a thick cloud destroy
The prison that containes: shee's returnd
Already.

[Enter **MILENA**.

What sayes Hippolito?

MILENA

Like an honest Gentleman, hee's at the graden gate.
I told him how things were at home, I met him
hard by, as if he meant without inviting
Having expected you so long, to come
Neerer, and waite some opportunitie
To speake with you.

CLARIANA

Th'art fortunate admit him, tis nor
Safe to expect there, but while we conferre
Vse thy best diligence round about to bring
If there be such misfortune, the first newes
Of Bellamente.

MILENA

Ile be carefull Madam.

[Exit.

CLARIANA

I m'e glad hees come
With what looke shall I first salute him?

[Re-enter **MILENA** with **HIPPOLITO**.

MILENA

Pray excuse me sir!

HIPPOLITO

Twill purchase but a paire of Gloves.

MILENA

I have him at my fingers ends, well I can but thinke
What serviceable creatures we Chambermaids are
Sometimes we are the best Cabinets for Ladies, and they
Trust their jewells of honor with us, but I must looke
About me, I know my office.

[Exit.

CLARIANA

Y'ave seene this face before, does it seeme strange?

HIPPOLITO

I have seene it, when it was lesse sad, but tis
The richer Iewell set in blacke, you never
Wore garments did so well become you Lady.

CLARIANA

I shall not love em'worse because they please
Your Eye, they fit the habit of my mind.

HIPPOLITO

Your voice has better musicke too, it sounds
As some religious melancholy strooke.
Vpon your heart y'aue praid lately I distinguish
A teare upon your cheeke still tis well done.

CLARIANA

If there be any signe of sorrow here
Tis for your sake.

HIPPOLITO

I cannot blame thy eyes,
If every time, I ame presented to 'em
Th' unhadpy obiect thou dost weepe Clariana,

I have deserved to find the lowest place
Within thy charity, yet such is thy
Compassion, when my fate is cast
And my unworthy life markd for the sacrifice
Thou art willing to preserve Hippolito
And to that purpose sentst to speake with me.

CLARIANA
You read my letter?

HIPPOLITO
Clariana, I
Shall not have time enough to thanke thee, when
Thou hast discovered what conspiracy
Threatens my head, unlesse you use some brevity
There is a worke this morning to be finished
Requires my personall attendance.

CLARIANA
I am.
Not ignorant what busnesse is designd
It was the reason of my zealous wishes
To change some words before.

HIPPOLITO
I waite your purpose.

CLARIANA
You are this morning to receive a wife.

HIPPOLITO
And such blessing as the earth were poore
Without her.

CLARIANA
Tis Eubella I understand.

HIPPOLITO
That most vertuous faire one.

CLARIANA
Ile not take from her
I have heard her much commended, but she is
No miracle.

HIPPOLITO
How Clariana.

CLARIANA

Our sex were poore
If she alone had all the grace of woman.
Though she be faire, the Dukedome is not so
Barren but it may shew some parralell.
And let it not be thought a pride, if I
Affirme there have beene those, have said as much
Of me, all beavty is not circumscrib'd
In one.

HIPPOLITO

You point at that which takes the Eye
And is but halfe a hansomnesse at best
Vnlesse the mind be furnished with those vertues
Which write a woman faire, but Clariana
There is no time for this dispute, and I
Am somewhat sorry you have falne upont
When I but praisd Eubella modestly,
She is to me the best and fairest now
Of all the world, but turne to the occasion
That brought me hither, I would heare what practise
Is meant against my life, which I would now
Preserue for that deere virgin, more then love
To keepe it for my use, I did imagine
How ever Bellamente shewed a formall
And calme release, yet he would meditate
Revenge at such a time he most should wound me
And had not I a perfect confidence
Your thoughts meant simple pitty to my danger
I should not thus farre have engaged my self,
Then I beseech you tell me.

CLARIANA

Any thing.

HIPPOLITO

Why dee delay me thus Clariana?

CLARIANA

Pardon o pardon me Hippolito
Indeed I will discover all the plot.

HIPPOLITO

I am prepard.

CLARIANA

But there is no misfortune
Leveld at you, the danger is all mine

And I but use this policy, to take
My last farewell, for I must never see
You married.

HIPPOLITO
You amaze me, what unhappinesse?
Will Bellamente be so cruell to thee
Having forgiven.

CLARIANA
A hand more severe.
Is armd against me.

HIPPOLITO
Is there no prevention

CLARIANA
It is within your mercy to do much.

HIPPOLITO
Pronounce then as much safety as my strength
Can give thee against any enemy be
But Bellamente, I have wounded him
Too much already, may I credit then
There is treachery ayming at my blood
Declare what man I must oppose in thy
Protection.

CLARIANA
No man.

HIPPOLITO
Y'are misticall.

CLARIANA
A woman is my enemy.

HIPPOLITO
There will be
No use of valour then.

CLARIANA
But much of love
If you resolve to save bleeding Clariana
Thou must oppose Eubella.

HIPPOLITO
What was that?

Kill my Eubella?

CLARIANA

It stretches not so farre, onely I beg
You would not marry her, and I shall live.

HIPPOLITO

Not marry her, why theres no steele can bring
So certaine and so violent a death,
Forsake Eubella now, now when shee's drest
My glorious bride, the Nuptiall ceremonie
And Priest expecting us, I know you speake not
In hope I should beleeve, you may as well
Bid me'commit a murder on my life
For this will kill her and we both are one.
Who hath instructed you to this?

CLARIANA

My love
My love that will not suffer me to know
Thou must be given thus away for ever
I could endure thy absence for whole yeeres
And not complaine, repent my equall sorrow
We have so farre offended, while you keepe
Your present freedome, there were then some hope
A possiblility, at last to meet
In new affections to redeeme the old
But thus my expectation is destroyd,
You understand?

HIPPOLITO

Too much, be not deceived,
There is no love that is not vertuous
And thy consenting thus farre but in thought
Is sacriledge, and thou dost rob the Church
Twice, first in violation of thy vowes
Which there were registred, and then mine expected
I dare not heare you talke thus.

CLARIANA

Is this all?
All the reward for loosing of my selfe
For thy sake?

HIPPOLITO

Y'are not yet quite lost.

CLARIANA

What curse
Made blacke the houre of my conception
Farewell Hippolito, when you heare me dead
Come to my grave, and drop one teare upon me

HIPPOLITO
What meanes Clariana?

[Enter **MILENA**, hastily.

MILENA
Oh Madam looke behind me
I see my Master comming in, and he
Suspecting my hast this way, followes me
With his sword drawne

[Enter **BELLAMENTE**.

BELLAMENTE
Are you so nimble? ha.

HIPPOLITO
Woman thou hast undone me.

CLARIANA
Oh my fortune againe betraid

BELLAMENTE
Nay then, Ile make sure worke

[Exit.

MILENA
Alas what shall become of me, the doores are lockt.

HIPPOLITO
Cruell dessembler.

CLARIANA
Hippolito the sequell shall acquit
My thoughts, Ime circled with more certaine danger
And cannot hope life.

HIPPOLITO
Tis not that I feare
To dy, thou knowst I am not guilty
Of any second shame, but my Eubella
That every minute lookes to be my bride

How the thought rends me.

CLARIANA
I can prevent his furie
Against thee.

HIPPOLITO
There is no way.

CLARIANA
Yes this.

[Draws a dagger andstabs him.

HIPPOLITO
Ha! divell what hast thou done?

[Wounds her with his sword.

MILENA
Alas what ha you both done?

CLARIANA
I thanke thee
Thou hast spar'd my execution on my selfe
Ile tell thee now Hippolito, by this
This crimson in whose ebbe my life hasts from me
I did not looke for Bellamente, but
Surprisd I thought it honor to beg in
The tragedy, I know my fate was not
To be resisted, twas impossible.
To find a second mercy from him, and
I would secure no woman after me.
Should boast the Conquest of Hippolito
Thy sword was gentle to me, search't againe
And thou shalt see.
How my embracing blood will keepe it warme
And kisse the kind destroyer.

[Falls.

[Enter **BELLAMENTE** and **SERVANTS**, **MILENA** runns in.

BELLAMENTE
What are you humbled? It must not serve your turne.

CLARIANA
We have deceivd your triumph.

HIPPOLITO

Bellamente.

CLARIANA

Heare me first, and know this bold hand sav'd
Thy fury to Hippolito, whom with
My last breath I pronounce not in a thought
Guilty of new dishonor.

BELLAMENTE

As soone perswade
It is not day.

HIPPOLITO

This letter summond me.

[Gives him the letter.

CLARIANA

I had no other meanes to speake with him
And my unruly love did prompt me to it.

HIPPOLITO

I tremble not in my innocence to thinke
Of death but my Eubella, poore Eubella.

CLARIANA

If she but lovd thee as I did, sheel'le follow
Furies will lend a torch to light her to
The shades we go to.

BELLAMENTE

Is the wickednesse all thine?

HIPPOLITO

Except the wound my hasty sword
Gave as reward for this too neere my heart
I feare.

CLARIANA

Dost feare?

HIPPOLITO

For poore Eubellas sake.

BELLAMENTE

Now thou hast met a justice in thy blood

For thy first sinne, but I will have a Surgeon.

HIPPOLITO
Send for Eubella rather
Oh let me breath my last upon her lips
It will concerne thee Bellamente somewhat
The world will think this murder was thine else.

BELLAMENTE
Make hast—

[Exit **SERVANT**.

O woman thou didst weepe once, when thy teares
Won my forgivenesse, where are all the drops,
The penitent showers, in which thy stained soule
Should bath it selfe, this minute lanching forth
To thy eternity.

CLARIANA
Th'are of another colour, oh forgive me
Good heaven, I have wrongd thee Bellamente
Oh wives hereafter, meane your hearts to them
You give your holy vowes, what mist weighs downe
My eyes already, oh tis death I see
In a long robe of darkenesse is preparing
To seale them up for ever, twere no death,
If we could loose our sinnes as we do breath.

[Dies.

BELLAMENTE
Shees gone to a long silence, place her body
There and then gently raise Hippolito
To the other chaire.

HIPPOLITO
Hast, hast my deare Eubella.

[Enter **BONALDO**.

BONALDO
How came this tragedy?

HIPPOLITO
Give me your last blessing
Ime going a long Pilgrimage, you gave
Too great a licence to my youth.

BONALDO
Howes this?

HIPPOLITO
My wanton bloud now payes fort, Clariana
And I have changd a wound, where is Eubella?

BONALDO
She is too neere this griefe, this punishment
Should ha beene mine long since, I was his father
In sinne as well as yeeres, she is dead already
Thy glasse had many sands till it was broken
Then those few minutes that are left of mine,
Ile number with my prayers.

[Enter **DUKE**, **EUBELLA**, **SEBASTIAN**, **COURTIERS**.

EUBELLA
Hippolito.

HIPPOLITO
My wound hath had a happy patience. Farewell.

[Dies. **EUBELLA** swoons.

SEBASTIAN
Eubella.

BONALDO
He is departed.

DUKE
Bellamente who hath done all this?

BELLAMENTE
Ile do my best to tell you
Here's all thats left of them whom how I lov'd,
Heaven and my poore heart knows.

EUBELLA
And is he slaine?
But once more let me kisse him.

BELLAMENTE
I did not kill em sir, they were too willing
To leave the world together, but their wrongs
All all the paiment for my honest love

awakd me to revenge, and had they beene
The very strings that tye my life together
It should ha falne to peeces, but their hands
Prevented mine.

DUKE
The cause? you rather leade me
To thinke you were their murderer, we must
Be better satisfied or your blood must answer
For this effusion.

BELLAMENTE
The cause my Lord—tis growne since it came hither
Pray give me leave, because you shanot suffer
Ith expectation, you shall have it all
Together, this Hippolito and that Clariana
Harke there tis.

[Falls and dies.

[Enter **MILENA**.

SEBASTIAN
His griefe has overchargd him.

DUKE
None to decipher these sad characters?

MILENA
With your pardon I can.

SEBASTIAN
Be comforted Eubella, all thy teares
Will not recall his life.

EUBELLA
Pray give me leave
Since he is dead to embalme him, had I di'ed
Before him, hee'd ha wept as much for me.

DUKE
We have heard too much but moderate Eubella,
Thy sorrows, he surviues that will supply
A bridegroome, and thy vertue bids me tender
My selfe a recompence for thy sufferings.

EUBELLA
I know you wod not lead me to forget

Hippolito so soone, I dare not thinke
Of being a Bride agen.

SEBASTIAN
Does your grace meane this honor?

DUKE
By my Duke dome.

SEBASTIAN
After this shower is over, she will shine
Doubt not my Lord, and blesse her happy starres

DUKE
Lead from this charvell house they shall be interrd
With all solemnity becomes there birth
And when their funerall rites and teares are done
New joyes shall rise with the next mornings Sunne.

[Exit **OMNES**.

FINIS.

JAMES SHIRLEY – A CONCISE BIBLIOGRAPHY

The following includes years of first publication, and of performance if known, together with dates of licensing by the Master of the Revels if available.

TRAGEDIES
The Maid's Revenge (licensed 9th February 1626; printed, 1639)
The Traitor (licensed 4th May 1631; printed, 1635)
Love's Cruelty (licensed 14th November 1631; printed, 1640)
The Politician (acted, 1639; printed, 1655)
The Cardinal (licensed 25th May 1641; printed, 1652).

TRAGI-COMEDIES
The Grateful Servant (licensed 3rd November 1629 as The Faithful Servant; printed 1630)
The Young Admiral (licensed 3rd July 1633; printed 1637)
The Coronation (licensed 6th February 1635, as Shirley's, but printed in 1640 as a work of John Fletcher)
The Duke's Mistress (licensed 18th January 1636; printed 1638)
The Gentleman of Venice (licensed 30th October 1639; printed 1655)
The Doubtful Heir (printed 1652), licensed as Rosania, or Love's Victory in 1640
The Imposture (licensed 10th November 1640; printed 1652)
The Court Secret (printed 1653).

COMEDIES

Love Tricks, or the School of Complement (licensed 10th February 1625; printed under its subtitle, 1631)
The Wedding (ca. 1626; printed 1629)
The Brothers (licensed 4th November 1626; printed 1652)
The Witty Fair One (licensed 3rd October 1628; printed 1633)
The Humorous Courtier (licensed 17th May 1631; printed 1640).
The Changes, or Love in a Maze (licensed 10th January 1632; printed 1639)
Hyde Park (licensed 20th April 1632; printed 1637)
The Ball (licensed 16th November 1632; printed 1639)
The Bird in a Cage, or The Beauties (licensed 21st January 1633; printed 1633)
The Gamester (licensed 11th November 1633; printed 1637)
The Example (licensed 24th June 1634; printed 1637)
The Opportunity (licensed 29th November 1634; printed 1640)
The Lady of Pleasure (licensed 15th October 1635; printed 1637)
The Royal Master (acted and printed 1638)
The Constant Maid, or Love Will Find Out the Way (printed 1640)
The Sisters (licensed 26th April 1642; printed 1653).
Honoria and Mammon (printed 1659)

DRAMAS
A Contention for Honor and Riches (printed 1633), morality play
The Triumph of Peace (licensed 3rd February 1634; printed 1634), masque
The Arcadia (printed 1640), pastoral tragicomedy
St. Patrick for Ireland (printed 1640), neo-miracle play
The Triumph of Beauty (ca. 1640; printed 1646), masque
The Contention of Ajax and Ulysses (printed 1659), entertainment
Cupid and Death (performed 26th March 1653; printed 1659), masque